DEMCO

A BRIEF INTRODUCTION
TO PIAGET

THE GROWTH OF UNDERSTANDING
IN THE YOUNG CHILD
NEW LIGHT ON CHILDREN'S IDEAS OF NUMBER

NATHAN ISAACS

Foreword by Evelyn Lawrence

SCHOCKEN BOOKS · NEW YORK

First SCHOCKEN PAPERBACK edition 1974

Second Printing, 1975

Copyright © 1960, 1961 by Nathan Isaacs
U. S. edition copyright © 1972 by Agathon Press, Inc.
Library of Congress Catalog Card No. 74–9738
Published by arrangement with Agathon Press
Manufactured in the United States of America

Library of Congress Cataloging in Publication Data

Isaacs, Nathan, 1895–1966
  A brief introduction to Piaget.

  Reprint of the ed. published by Agathon Press and distributed by Schocken
Books, New York.
  CONTENTS: The growth of understanding in the young child.—New
light on children's ideas of number.—Publisher's bibliography (p.   ).
  1. Piaget, Jean, 1896–   . I. Isaacs, Nathan, 1895–1966. New light on
children's ideas of number. 1974. II. Title.
[LB775.P4918 1974]   155.4'13   74–9738

TABLE OF CONTENTS

FOREWORD

Nathan Isaacs was born in 1895 at Frankfurt-am-Main, of a Russian-Jewish rabbinical family. His father had broken away from the faith and from his village on the Polish border, and had become a wandering scholar, with little success in either the business side of the wandering or the scholarship. A Hebrew dictionary at which he worked all his life never found a publisher.

After a childhood spent mainly in Switzerland, Nathan went at the age of twelve to London, which then became the family home. At the age of fourteen he joined the ranks of bowler-hatted businessmen, working in a metal merchant's firm. He worked very successfully at his job by day and acquired an education at night. The foundation for this study had been laid in his domestic atmosphere and in his schooling at the Basel Gymnasium.

With the outbreak of the first world war he managed to enlist in the British army. This was somewhat difficult as the authorities looked rather doubtfully at a candidate whose nationality was Russian and whose birthplace was Germany. However, he did join the army and was badly gassed in the trenches, with consequences to his health which were to last all his life.

Soon after the war he joined an evening class in psychology at which Susan Brierley was the lecturer. He startled her by presenting her with a 95-page essay so far outside the usual students' calibre that she realized immediately she had caught a whale in her herring net. Before very long they married, and began the partnership which resulted in a joint contribution to British educational psychology of inestimable value.

At this stage Nathan Isaacs' main intellectual interest was in philosophy, especially in logic, epistemology and ethics. However, though he joined the Aristotelian Society and attended meetings regularly, he was entirely dissatisfied with the methods, the vocabulary and the ways of thinking of academic philosophers. He considered most of their subject matter not pure philosophy at all, but a mixture of philosophy and inadequate, outdated psychology which they did not even recognize as such. He worked for years on a long book setting out his theory of knowledge as a temporal distillation of experience, continually corrected by the confirmation or non-confirmation of expectation. He made no attempt to publish the work at this time.

Early in the 1920s Geoffrey Pike invited Susan Isaacs to run an experimental school for young children at his home in Cambridge, and the three founders, Pike, and Nathan and Susan Isaacs thrashed out together the theoretical basis on which the school would run. Susan's psychoanalytical training gave her a special interest in the conditions for optimum emotional development; her husband, influenced partly by J. M. Baldwin's *Genetic Logic*, was insistent that from the earliest years children should be encouraged to think clearly and talk competently. Unless these faculties were actively developed from the very start of education, he felt, the muddled thinking and cliché-ridden opinions which pass from one generation to the next would persist indefinitely.

The ambitious plans which underlay the foundation of the little Malting House School embraced expansion to an all-age school which would carry on the methods through the whole of childhood. Essential to the philosophy was that the children's real interests should form the basic platform for learning.

The school would demonstrate what could be accomplished in the lifetime of a single generation by correctly placed emphasis in the vital early stages. But the experiment did not last for long. After a very few years Geoffrey Pike's fortune which was to finance it melted away, and the school had to be abandoned. But it was the material carefully recorded during the life of the school which formed the basis of Susan Isaacs' two books, *Intellectual Growth in Young Children* and *Social Development in Young Children.* Nathan Isaacs was intimately involved in their planning. His appendix on *Children's Why Questions* was an important contribution. These two volumes have become classics of primary school education, translated into many languages.

It was Nathan Isaacs who persuaded his wife to accept an invitation to inaugurate the Child Development Department at the London University Institute of Education. Until then the universities had held firmly to the view that the education of young children was none of their business. The Isaacs were acquainted, at this time, with the early work of Piaget but they were critical of his method and did not then consider that he had much to offer to their own educational thinking.

During all this time Nathan Isaacs had been earning his living in the metal trade. When the second world war came he went on temporary duty with the civil service, working in the Ministry of Supply as organizer of the acquisition and distribution of the rare minerals needed for the war effort. For this responsibility he was later awarded the Order of the British Empire. The task had been too heavy and exacting for any other activity to be possible, but as soon as he was back in ordinary life he returned to his double occupation of business and scholarship.

Susan Isaacs died in 1948, and the long partnership in intellectual effort ended. Susan had always had the greater power of simple exposition for the ordinary reader, but she intensely valued Nathan's relentless logical criticism. Nathan at this stage was a difficult author. His swift flow of abstract thought, unrelieved by examples of what he was talking about, meant that his readers were respectful but rather few. But he worked very hard at reducing his epistemological book in size and making it more readable. It was published in 1949 as *The Foundations of Common Sense*. There was no sign that it made instant converts among the philosophers, as his admirers thought it ought to have done, but it was recognized as a highly interesting piece of original thought.

From this time the direction of Nathan Isaacs' efforts changed somewhat. He joined the governing body of the National Froebel Foundation, which for a hundred years or so under differing titles had been concerned with liberalizing and improving the education of young children. He became more involved with what was being done in the ordinary schools, and wrote for and lectured to teachers. By now a further series of Piaget's books had been issued, though most of them had not yet been translated. Nathan Isaacs realized that the methodology was now more acceptable to him, and that a momentous step forward had been taken by this work, both for psychology and for education. In 1955 the Froebel Foundation published a summary in English of *The Child's Conception of Number*, followed by an analysis of this and an article on its bearing on the education of young children. It was from this beginning that the great interest among teachers in Piaget's work largely started.

During all his last years Nathan Isaacs was a kind of elder statesman in the field of early childhood education, much sought after not only for adding theoretical weight when the cause of progressive education had to be argued, but also as a superb critic of other people's work. No logical error could evade his scrutiny. The two essays reprinted here were the result of great effort on his part to put the case in a form which he found logically satisfactory while at the same time rendering Piaget's difficult thought and vocabulary into a form easily assimilated by teachers.

This work for teachers did not mean that he had turned

away from his own earlier interests. In most ways he was always ahead of his time. A leading article in *Nature* in 1927 had drawn the attention of scientists to the importance of encouraging the earliest stirrings of interest in quite small children in the how and why of natural events. In 1931 he had read a paper called "Psychologic" to the Aristotelian Society, decades before this term was widely adopted by linguists. His last work with the National Froebel Foundation, before he died in 1966, was helping to collect and evaluate records kept by a number of practising teachers of "discovery" methods in their classes.

EVELYN LAWRENCE
1972

THE GROWTH
OF UNDERSTANDING
IN THE YOUNG CHILD

I

INTRODUCTION

1. THE GREAT IMPORTANCE of the work of Professor Jean Piaget of Geneva for child psychology, and thus for education, has only in recent years been fully recognized. This work has gone on for some thirty-five years, but the sequence of books translated between 1927 and 1932, though very stimulating, seemed open to a good many doubts. However, the volumes published in English during the last decade, and others still untranslated, have shown beyond question how much Professor Piaget can help us to understand children's intellectual growth. We owe to him a striking fresh picture of the child himself as the architect of this growth. Piaget's interest lies chiefly in the building-up of the basic framework of thought, which later the child, and we, mostly take for granted; but that is what makes the new picture so illuminating. And from the angle of Infant School teachers it is noteworthy that the period from 4–5 years to 7–8 years turns out to be a specially important one, anyway for the average run of children. For their biggest step forward in the building of that framework usually falls within this period. The present essay will offer a thumbnail sketch of the whole story, as Piaget presents it, and will then dwell more fully on the happenings of the Infant School phase.

2. The sketch must be very "thumbnail" indeed, because of the sheer mass of Piaget's work. Since about 1935 it has been based on systematic experiments, carried out not only by Piaget himself but also by colleagues operating under his

direction, and many teams of students. There are over a dozen volumes reporting experimental findings from 1935 onward, besides numerous articles by Piaget, and many semi-independent researches carried on at his Institute in recent years. Some of these volumes will be referred to later, but nothing more than sample soundings can be offered here. It is, however, worth adding that in the last few years various other workers in England have repeated sections of Piaget's investigations and mainly confirmed his results. A case of particular interest to working teachers is that of a headmaster who read Piaget's book on the Child's Conception of Number, and, like many others, found its contents, in his own telling phrase, "either incomprehensible or incredible". However, he proceeded right away to try out most of the experiments in his own school, obtained the same "incredible" results and went on, in their light, to revise the school's ways of handling its arithmetic teaching. The responses were very encouraging and the experiment is going on.

3. This brings out two further points of which readers should be warned: (i) Piaget's books are in general very difficult to read; his "theory" is usually presented in a highly abstract and technical vocabulary. This is a great pity and whilst anyone undismayed by the difficulties is amply rewarded, many working teachers may well have to wait till an "Ordinary Reader's Guide to Piaget" sees the light of day. However, some few references which may prove helpful are listed on page 57* (ii) The actual experiments are usually as concrete as any child could wish and represent play situations into which even 4–5 year olds enter with ready interest. But just this fact makes the children's failures, their flat contradictions and sheer absurdities, startling to the reader who has not previously come up against these uncharted areas of small children's minds. One's first impulse is to find fault with the experiments, or anyway with this or that feature in

---

* See, however, the publisher's bibliography, starting on p. 119.

them; but presently one notes that Piaget had foreseen one's criticisms and varied his procedure, whilst still obtaining the same results. Also a few pages later one meets children on the average only 6–12 months older who are in an obvious half-way phase, sometimes getting the easier results right, sometimes falling back into the same absurdities; whilst another 6–12 months on, the children tested are astonished at such infantile questions, and offer the answers one would expect. Moreover, as already remarked, the experiments have been independently repeated with similar results. Thus it is the very surprise-effect of Piaget's findings which measures their revealingness and shows how much new psychological understanding is to be learnt from them.

II

THE PIAGETIAN PICTURE
OF THE CHILD'S DEVELOPMENT

1. KEYS TO THE CHILD'S MENTAL GROWTH

THE MAIN KEYS to the child's mental growth, as Piaget brings them out, are (i) the paramount part played from the start by his own *action* (ii) the way this turns into a process of *inward building-up,* that is, of forming within his mind a continually extending *structure* corresponding to the world outside.

(i) *The child as agent*

(a) Piaget shows how from the beginning, the infant himself takes a controlling hand in procuring and organizing all his experience of the outside world. He follows with his eyes, explores with them, turns his head; explores with his hands, grips, lets go, pulls, pushes; explores with his mouth; moves his body and limbs; explores jointly and alternately with eye and hand, etc. All this brings experiences which come to him as the products of his activities and are formed into psychic schemes or patterns *keyed* by them. That keying becomes even more clearly marked when, happening upon an interesting experience, he is stimulated to repeat the activity that led to it, and then *goes on* with it or, after an interval, returns to it. This process of absorbing and organizing experiences round the activities that produce them Piaget calls *"assimilation"*. He regards it as our most fundamental process of learning and growth, which indeed goes on for the rest of our lives. However, assimilation is always being modified by an accompanying process of *accommodation.* Many situations or objects resist the activity patterns the child tries on them, and in so doing impose some changes on these patterns themselves. Still others yield *new* results which go to enrich the range or scope of the patterns.

Thus the assimilative processes constantly extend their domain whilst at the same time accommodation steers them into ever more successful *adaptation* to the world. This dual process, and the endeavour to maintain an equal balance between the two sides, are for Piaget the chief controlling factors of intellectual growth.

(b) To begin with, the activities that organize patterns of resulting experiences round them can only be physical, directed to outward objects and situations. Their scope indeed widens all the time, as the child's powers grow and above all as he masters locomotion and his range of exploration and action is thus immensely multiplied. But in the course of the second year, these external activities also develop a great new inward dimension. Language comes in and with it a more and more settled power of evocation and representation of absent things. This power is the main foundation for the unfolding activity of thought. The latter begins essentially as a form of *action in terms of internal images,* and presently of their verbal symbols, extending the range of the child's *physical action on outward objects.* Thought is in fact for Piaget just action carried on inwardly and thus started on a new career of internal organization and growth.

(c) That story goes on developing through all the child's activities, outward and inward, during the next few years; but his most decisive advance usually comes only towards 7–8, when, by various related moves forward, he establishes himself on the level of *structured thinking.* This Piaget calls the stage of *concrete* operations of thought, because it still remains tied to tangible starting-points and goals, taken over from the real world. In the years that follow, the child exploits and consolidates these newfound powers of controlled thinking; but at the same time he prepares the ground for his next and final advance. Between 11 and 14 he attains the power of *abstract* thought—that is, thought emancipated from the given facts of the real world and able to operate freely with its own imagined possibilities and hypotheses. It can work out the logical consequences of these, or vary them or even reverse them, and draw a fresh set of consequences. How much use the child makes of this ability will depend on his bent, interests and native capacity; but in suitable subjects it can lead all the way to the most abstruse forms of logical, mathematical or scientific thought. Yet the link with action remains unbroken. All thought, as Piaget sees it, is operation, and operation is internalized action; it is this that determines the whole of our human experience, all our thought-life and learning, and all human mental growth.

(ii) *The child as inward builder*

Piaget thus directs our attention to what in fact lies behind our characteristic behaviour as human beings. Right from the start we build up in our minds a kind of working model of the world around us; in other words, a model of a world of persisting and moving objects and recurring happenings set in a framework of space and time and showing a regular order. As will be described presently, Piaget shows how far this model-building is carried, in a functional yet unmistakable way, even in our first eighteen months, that is, prior to the help of language or explicit thought. Once the basic model is in our minds, the rest is merely a matter of building on, filling in and organizing; the structure remains the same, even though it is immeasurably expanded and enriched. In fact we carry it with us for the rest of our lives and although we normally take it for granted, it continually *regulates* all our planning and action. We are drawing on it—and relying upon it—whenever we start to *think out* any course of action: its space aspect when we want to get somewhere; its scheme of material objects when we want to make or construct something; its order of events, when we want to bring about or to prevent some happening.

From the appropriate part of the model in our minds we then work out the actual sequence of movements or actions which we shall have to follow. In a great number of cases this process is virtually automatic; our purposes bring into our thoughts the programmes needed to give effect to them, and we get on with these without worrying how we have come by them. If, however, we stumble on a difficulty and need to stop for some real thinking, this may well make us explicitly aware, first, of the scheme in our minds which has carried us so far, secondly of the nature of the present gap in it, and thirdly of what help we might be able to get from bringing further parts of our thought-resources to bear.

If then we consider the whole range of planned courses of action on which we constantly launch ourselves, we can get some measure of the connected and organized scheme of things in our minds on which they must rest. Our plans of course always contemplate the real world itself, in which they are to be realized; but the point is that when we are making them, we are *fore*seeing, *fore*thinking and *fore*planning, and can therefore only be doing so from the model of that real world in our *minds*. We are naturally thinking of the real world, but at that stage we are only *thinking* of it. However our model so truly corresponds to it, at any rate in its main structure, that we can pass straight over from the model to the real world without any further thought. It is only in matters of comparative detail that it is liable to prove wrong or insufficient.

Piaget's work can greatly help us to grasp this situation, since it shows more clearly than anything before just how we build up that structured model of the world in our minds. We are not born with it, but have to construct it piecemeal, right from its foundations. Piaget demonstrates in detail how the child does this, from the first few weeks of his life onward. Here is the briefest outline of the process as he exhibits it.

2. THE MAIN BUILDING STAGES

(i) *First 18 months; sensori-motor phase*

Through a series of revealing tests on his own three in-fants, Piaget brings out the stages by which the first building-up proceeds. The earliest behaviour shows not the least sense of persisting objects or of the most rudimentary space or time relations. But presently it is seen to change, and month by month it takes more account of these features of the world, until the child clearly has in his mind a scheme that corre-sponds to them. We see him *recognizing* different objects as such and expecting them to persist, to move in space and to display spatial characters and relations. Similarly he *recog-nizes* different happenings and expects them to take a certain course, expects some of them to lead on to others, and so on. The infant's conduct is now visibly *pre*-adjusted to all this; i.e. it is controlled by something in his mind which regularly anticipates just those features. How he is led to form that controlling schema has already been referred to; he learns by doing and trying, by assimilating all the different experiences that thus come to him, and by constantly varying and ex-tending his experimental activities. And by eighteen months the range and variety of his purposive behaviour already bears witness to the controlling presence in his mind of the sort of basic world-model I have described.

(ii) *18 months to 4–5 years: stage of intuitive thought*

So much having already been achieved, the child has only to go on to exploit all the further instruments and powers that come to him. He now incessantly expands and enriches, works over, organizes and re-organizes, his inward model of the world. He does so mainly through imaginative play on the one hand and through more exploring and experi-menting, combined with questioning, listening and talking, on the other hand. The different kinds of objects and happenings which he can recognize, pre-adjust to, remember and imagine continually increase, whilst at the same time his sense of space-relations and time-relations becomes more varied and better articulated. Yet most of the detailed images and ideas in his mind tend to remain vague and unstable, and his thinking cannot move away from present situations without losing itself.

(iii) *4–5 years to 7–8 years: advance to stage of concrete operations*

Piaget now concentrates above all on the state of the child's main *frame-work* notions and what happens to them. Thus he examines how children progress in their notions of different aspects of space, of time, of movement and speed, of number and measure, and of elementary logical relations such as those of whole and part, classes and sub-classes, or serial order, etc. By numerous experiments he shows that most 4–5 year olds of average intelligence have as yet no settled notions in any of these fields. Everything is still in a state of flux, nothing is clear or stays put. Size, shape, arrangement, etc. are mixed up with number; distance and length with movement; rate of movement with overtaking or catching up; time with speed, and so on.

The same experiments, however, carried out with children only about a year older show the *beginnings* of a notable change. At least in the simpler cases they can, by trial and error, sort their ideas out, and thus get some first inklings of the true meaning of distance, length, number and the rest. Thereafter there is usually further piecemeal progress and then, perhaps another year on, the scene is transformed. By 7–8 years children deal with most of the concrete experimental situations much as an ordinary adult would. Each of the basic structural concepts is now clear and stable. In Piaget's language, the level of "conservation" has been reached. That is, distance, length, number, speed, mass, class-inclusion, etc., now each stand for something *constant,* whichever way round it is taken, however it is subdivided, and, in the case of number, however it is arranged in space, concentrated or spread. Moreover we have here concepts that can be linked together in larger structures which in turn have the same character of conservation. In fact various sets of these concepts taken together come to form distinctive schemes of operational thought. That means, schemes of connected relational *reasoning,* either mathematical or logical, such as eventually make up geometry, arithmetic, mathematics at large, mechanics, and the formal logical aspects of all other sciences. That may seem to be looking a long way ahead, and is not properly realized till the stage of full abstract reasoning is reached at 11–14 years. What Piaget establishes, however, is that the first prototypes of these operational ideas, that is, concepts that possess the minimum characters needed, are present in most children's minds from the age of 7–8 years. Thus the basic structure of their world is now properly laid down in their thought, not of course in words, but in functioning ideas. Therefore they can think out, flexibly and successfully, the simple everyday space relations (distances, sizes, etc.), time-relations (intervals, successions, overlaps, etc.), or mechanical, numerical and logical relations which we all continually need. How far they have had to travel in order to get to this level is shown in the most illuminating way by Piaget's work on the earlier stages, from about 4–5 years onward.

III

THE CONCEPT OF NUMBER

ALL THIS LONG struggle forward in children's thinking comes out very clearly in the development of their number ideas— the part of Piaget's work which is now best known in this country. It offers a striking illustration both of the nature of his discoveries and of the basic pattern of mental growth. We can watch how the child starts from a level of utter confusion, without a notion of what number really means even though he may be able to count to ten or twenty; a level where number is completely mixed up with size, shape and arrangement, or constantly shifts according to the way it is subdivided or added up. And we can see how, on an average two years later, children declare of their own accord that a number *must* stay the same, whatever you do with it, so long as you do not actually add to it or take away from it; or that whatever you have done with it, you can always reverse this and get back to where you started from; or that you can always show it to be the same by counting; and so on.

The following are a few examples of the ways in which Piaget's experiments bring out this pattern of growth:

1. Each child was presented with *two* vessels of the same shape and size containing equal quantities of coloured liquid. Then the contents of one of them was poured into (a) two similar but smaller vessels, (b) several such, (c) a tall but narrow vessel, (d) a broad but shallow one. In each case the child was asked whether the quantity of liquid was still the same as in the untouched vessel.

Piaget found that at a first stage, around 4–5 years, children took it for granted that the quantity of liquid was now *different*—either more because the level was higher, or more because there were more glasses, or less because the new vessel was narrower, or less because the levels in the two or more glasses were lower. In other words, there was no idea of a constant quantity, independent of its changing forms; if its appearance changed, the quantity changed and could become either more or less according to what aspect of the new appearance caught the child's eye. At a second stage, at about 5½–6, children had reached a transitional phase, in which they wavered uncertainly between the visual appearances and the dawning idea of conservation in their minds. Thus the quantity of liquid might be regarded as still the same when it was poured into *two* smaller glasses, but as greater when it was poured into *three*. Or as remaining the same if the difference in level or cross-section in the new vessel was small, but not if it was larger. Or the child might *try* to allow for the relation between cross-section and level, and experiment uncertainly without reaching any clear conclusion. In the third stage, between 6½ and 8, children give the correct answers right away, either by reference to the height-width relation, or by pointing out that the quantity has not been changed: "It's only been poured out".

2. As a check on these results, Piaget carried out a similar set of experiments, with beads instead of liquids. In this way something close to counting could be introduced (e.g. the child putting beads into a container one by one as the experimenter did the same into another vessel). Also he could be asked to imagine that the beads inside each vessel were arranged into the familiar shape of a necklace. The outcome was entirely the same. At the first stage, the children thought that the quantity of beads would be either more or less, and would make a longer or shorter necklace, according as the level looked higher, or the width greater, or there were more vessels, and this happened even when a child had put one

bead into his vessel for each one that the experimenter placed in his. At stage 2 there is a struggle in the child's mind as before. This may show itself for example by his first going wrong when comparing levels between a wider and a taller vessel; then correcting himself if asked to think in terms of the necklaces; but when the beads are spread over two or more containers, still thinking that the necklace will be longer. At stage 3 once more the children reply correctly and cannot be shaken, however the questions or the experiments may be varied.

3. The next experiments were intended to test whether children could match two sets of objects against one another, and could then *hold on* to this equality as something conserved or constant. Thus they were asked to tally eggs with eggcups, bottles with glasses, vases with flowers, or to buy so many flowers with so many coins at a flower per coin.

For example, six small bottles were put on a table and the child was offered a tray of say 10 glasses and asked to place a glass by each bottle. The 4–5 year olds at stage 1 took an arbitrary number of glasses, or all of them, and even then, through arranging them much closer together than the bottles, concluded that there were more bottles than glasses. At stage 2 (up to about 6 years) the matching gave no difficulty, but if the experimenter brought the glasses closer together than the bottles, the children found more bottles than glasses. If then the glasses were spread out further, they found more of these than bottles. They could not be shifted from these beliefs, whatever changes were rung on the situation, including even getting a child to count off, first six bottles and then six glasses. At stage 3 (illustrated here by one child of $5\frac{1}{2}$ and another of $6\frac{2}{12}$) the right answer is given at once, whatever the experimenter does, and he is told that he has "only put the bottles close together", etc.

The flower-and-vase and eggcup-and-egg experiment proved somewhat easier because the children were more used to matching these objects; but apart from rather quicker progress, the character of the responses was much the same.

The exchange of flowers for coins one by one presented no difficulties even at stage 1. But when it was completed and the coins put in a row whilst the flowers were bunched—or else the flowers in a row and the coins piled up—there were either more coins than flowers or more flowers than coins. At stage 2 the sole progress was that children no longer had to proceed one by one, but could match four coins against four flowers, or seven against seven. But the moment the visual correspondence was disturbed, the equivalence was lost again. At stage 3 (one case as young as $4\frac{11}{12}$) equality was firmly insisted upon, whatever the visual appearance, either because it could be restored by matching, or because once it had been created, it was *there* ("Because I gave you my pennies").

4. As another test of a similar order, children were presented with various patterns formed from counters, and asked to pick out of a box the same number of counters. The patterns chosen were (a) a random array, (b) two parallel rows, (c) closed figures like a circle or a house, (d) closed figures based on a fixed small number of counters, e.g. a square, a cross, etc., (e) more complex and less familiar figures, like a rhombus.

At stage 1 there are only what Piaget calls "global qualitative comparisons", or "rough reproductions of the configuration of the models". At stage 2 the children still try to reproduce the model, but now do so counter for counter. However, if the resulting shape is changed, equality vanishes, though they have themselves just established it on a one to one basis. At stage 3 they no longer depend on reproducing the figures, but if necessary break these up and arrange them in a series, to make sure that they arrive at the right number of counters.

By way of a further variant of these tests, children were shown a row of six beans, representing sweets or coins, and asked to pick the same number from a pile. Here again the stage 1 subjects go by either the length of the row, or its density, but have no thought of co-ordinating the two. Thus a child might put down 10 beans as equal to 6, then notice that the 10 made a shorter row and add some more. If the 6 were spread out further, he would keep adding, but if they were closed up and his new row spread out, he would say "Now *I* have more" . . . On the other hand there were those who went by the density and thought that 6 were more than 7 "because they're close together; there are a lot". At stage 2 the children could get as far as picking the correct number and setting it over against the model, but if either row was then spaced out or closed up, the equality would again be denied. At stage 3 the right number is picked and placed in a shorter or longer row, or just heaped up, without any regard for what is done to the model.

5. Experiments to test whether children have grasped the arithmetical relation of parts to a whole, or of equal parts:

(i) They were handed four beans to represent four sweets for the morning break, and another four intended for tea-time. After that two more lots of four were put in front of them and they were told that these were for tomorrow, but they would only eat one in the morning and save all the others for tea-time. As they watched, three sweets would be taken away from one of these sets and added to the other. The children would then be asked to compare the two (4 + 4 and 1 + 7), and say whether they would be eating the same number tomorrow as to-day. At stage 1 they will consider 7 + 1 either more or less than 4 + 4, according as they compare the 7 or the 1 with the 4's in the other group, but they will not see them as equal. At stage 2 children begin the same way, but gradually realize that although 7 is greater than 4, there is also 1 which is less than 4 and that this should act as a set-off. At stage 3 that is now self-evident. The members of each set have become units, which, however grouped, make up the same total, since one set grows as the other shrinks. Addition and subtraction are now *understood*.

(ii) Two unequal groups of counters (8 and 14) were shown and the children asked to make them equal by shifting units from one to the other (combined addition and subtraction). At stage 1 they just take some from the larger set and add them to the other, or else keep moving counters backward and forward, with an eye only on the smaller lot, and no idea that increasing the one means decreasing the other. At stage 2 children think up the notion of arranging the counters in comparable figures, say circles, with a few in the middle, but if the figure is altered in any way, the equality they have themselves established vanishes again. At stage 3 they deliberately pair off the counters and then divide the difference.

(iii) Children were asked to share out a heap of counters equally between two people. At stage 1, they would make a rough division, but though this might chance to be right, they would think it wrong if one lot took up more space than the other. Or they might even deal out the counters one by one, and still think the two lots unequal if one looked larger or smaller. At stage 2, they would expressly build up two matching rows (or other figures) but again deny this equality as soon as the spacing was altered. At stage 3 they would share out their counters one or two at a time into equal sets, and no re-arrangement could put them off, because they had "put the same on both sides".

The foregoing covers only a limited part of the test situations described in "The Child's Conception of Number". Besides others dealing with cardinal numbers, there is an interesting sequence concerned with serial arrangements, and with ordinal numbers and their relation to cardinal ones. There are also tests of children's understanding of the *logical* relation between a whole and its parts, as distinct from the *arithmetical* one, but bringing out the close kinship of the two. The main aim of the entire volume is to demonstrate what it takes for children to get the *real meaning* of number, that is, to separate this out from shape and size, spacing and arrangement and to place it in its own distinctive realm. That realm is one in which—as the child has to discover—each number conserves its own character, however much it may be taken apart and then put together again differently, or however it may be subdivided or grouped and re-grouped. But at the same time all the numbers belong together in one number scheme and are made up by the same operations. These operations of counting and adding and subtracting (and, later, their more complicated and powerful forms: multiplying and dividing) can be combined at will, taken in any order, and above all, they can always be "done the other way round", or *reversed*. That (as the child finds) is the very nature of the relation between addition and subtraction, and similarly between multiplication and division. In fact, it lies behind the persistence or conservation of all the separate numbers, each of which can be thought of as a permanent junction point for a different set of combining or balancing operations.

This is the kind of operational notion of number which the child has to achieve—and which, on the average between about $6\frac{1}{2}$ and 8 years, he does attain, anyway for those lower numbers that he can easily handle in his mind. In ordinary children of 4–5, there is not a trace of such a notion (even though they may be able to count freely to 10 or even 20); and any attempt to convey it to them meets with blank incomprehension or firm rejection. At an average age of 5–6 there are only tentative beginnings, and some first ability to respond to reiterated suggestions or promptings. Yet in children only 1–2 years older the whole basic idea is there. On the lower number level (that is, where the child does not get lost among unfamiliar symbols), he can now handle the various numerical relations as the situation demands. He can see, for example, how a number like 12 can be split up in the most various ways and yet stays the same 12 all the way through. And he can sweep aside all the non-numerical irrelevancies, like spacing, shape, size, etc. which a year or two earlier so confused him and defeated his number sense. The idea of number and all the operations connected with it now forms in fact an organized scheme in his mind under a single control.

Of course this remains a functional or working achievement, not a verbal one. The child can correctly *use* the notion of number and bring to bear the relations he needs, but he would not be able to put into formal words the principles that direct his practice. That, however, is not the important thing. Indeed, these principles—the "conservation of number", or "associativity", or "reversibility"—would mean nothing, if expressed in these terms, even to good arithmeticians among ordinary adults. What does matter is that the child's real grasp of the "number" idea will usually be limited to the figures he is familiar with in daily life, and there will be little or nothing to link up this grasp with his school arithmetic. For that most often only consists for him in a lot of "rules", mechanically learnt and not at all digested or understood; and he may never get beyond that stage. Whereas of course the *object* of his school arithmetic should be to make all the rules, and all the more complicated ways of handling numbers, *grow* out of his own grasp of the underlying idea. If that were to be the aim, the very first task would clearly be to help the child to master this *idea* (in terms naturally of the easy small numbers). For that purpose no time or trouble would be too much, and there would be no thought of going further until it was accomplished.

That brings me to the threshold of what Piaget's findings imply for education. Before I turn to this theme, however, let me try to illustrate very breifly the range of his work on some of our other main "framework" ideas.

IV

CHILDREN'S BASIC NOTIONS
ABOUT SPACE,
MOVEMENT AND TIME

I CAN ONLY GIVE a few simplified *samples,* since on the subject of space alone Piaget has two large volumes of experimental investigations, whilst "Movement and Speed" and "Time" fill two more books.

1. THE NOTION OF DISTANCE

Two dolls or toy trees of equal height are placed 50 cm. away from one another. (i) A cardboard screen, slightly higher, is set up between them and the children are asked whether the original figures are still as near one another, or as far apart, as they were before. (ii) They are also asked whether it is as far (or near) from the first figure to the second as from the second to the first. The experiment is varied by making one of the figures twice the height of the other, and again by raising one of them some 50 cm. above the level of the other.

At stage 1 (4–5 years), if the questions are understood, the screen is sometimes thought to bring the two figures nearer to one another, but most often the child just substitutes the distance to the screen for the total distance between the figures.

In his reply to the second question, he thinks the distance greater one way than the other because the second doll is "far away", or is "taller" or "high up".

At stage 2 (5–7 years) there is a first phase in which the distance is no longer broken up by the screen, but is thought to be shortened to the extent of its thickness. Furthermore, it still tends to be regarded as greater in one direction than in the other.

In a later phase, there are two intermediate responses: (i) the distance may now be the same when reckoned from either end, but if a screen is interposed, this still alters it; (ii) the screen no longer affects it, but it still varies according to the end from which it is taken, especially if one figure is higher than the other. Either way, the notion of distance as such, based on a single containing space, is not achieved yet; it still turns on the standpoint of the speaker, what he is seeing, the effort he would have to make, etc.

At stage 3 (from 7 years onward) the questions are at once correctly answered and distance is not affected by interpolated objects, by the direction in which it is measured, or by any other extraneous factor.

2. THE NOTION OF LENGTH

(i) Children have before them a horizontal straight stick and underneath it a length of wavy plasticine with its two ends in line with those of the stick. They have to say whether these are the same length or whether one is longer than the other.

At stage 1, up to $4\frac{1}{2}$ years, most of the children are positive that the length is the same. This applies even after they have been invited to follow the windings of the plasticine "snake" with their fingers. Furthermore when it is straightened out for them, they see it to be longer, but the moment it is bent into wave shape again, they once more call the length the same. In one case a child begins by saying that the "snake" is *shorter,* because it is "twisted", but after seeing it to be actually *longer,* he decides, when it is bent again, that the two lengths are the same.

At the beginning of stage 2 ($4\frac{1}{2}$–5 years) children still, for a start, consider only the end-points and judge the two lengths equal. However when they follow the winding line with their fingers, or are asked to picture somebody walking along it, they see that it is longer (though they may presently go back to their original judgment). By the end of stage 2 ($5\frac{1}{2}$–7 years) they straighten the "snake" out themselves in their minds and thus discover its greater length.

(ii) Children are shown two straight rods of say 5 cm. each, with their ends in line, and have no difficulty in seeing that they are the same length. One is then moved to project 1–2 cm. beyond the other, and they are asked which is longer, or whether they are the same length.

At stage 1 ($4\frac{1}{2}$–6 years) the projecting rod is found longer, and one five-year-old, when the relation of the two rods has been reversed, holds that they are *both* longer. (Length is identified with "reaching further"; the projection is followed with the eye and only the projecting end is attended to.)

At stage 2 (5–$7\frac{1}{2}$ years) there is every sort of intermediate reaction, shifting of ground, indecision, etc., but the correct answer gradually prevails. (A child of $6\frac{10}{12}$ says that if one looks at one rod, that seems longer, but if at the other rod, then that one. However, when he is asked "And if one looks at both", he replies "Then it's the same thing" and sticks to this.)

At stage 3 ($6\frac{1}{2}$–$7\frac{1}{2}$ years) the child at once gives the right reply for the right reasons (pointing to the space left unoccupied; or remarking that one rod projects one way, the other the other way, or that one rod has just been *shifted;* or commenting "still the same, the rods can't grow!")

3. THE NOTION OF AN AREA

To test children's grasp of this notion, a situation is devised in which equal areas are subtracted from equal areas and the child has to say whether the spaces left over are the same.

Two rectangular cardboard sheets, about 20 × 30 cm., are coloured green to represent two fields. Each has by its side a wooden cow which will be eating the grass. The child recognizes that the two cows will have the same amount of grass to eat. A wooden house is put down in the *middle* of one field, so that one cow has less grass than the other, but another house of the same size is now placed in a *corner* of the other field, and the question is put whether the two cows have the same amount of grass again. More houses are put down, one for one, in each field, but in the first they are scattered over the middle, whilst in the second they are put close to each other in the same corner. The child has to say each time whether the cows still have the same amount of grass, and this may be continued till there are 15 to 20 houses in each field; children have been found to reply "yes" up to 14 houses each, and then suddenly to fail because the visual difference has become too big for them.

At stage 1 not enough interest can usually be aroused for the experiment to continue. At stage 2a (5–5½ years) children are sure that the amount of grass left is *not* the same, from the first two houses onward. This may happen even if at first both are put down in the middle, and then, after the child has agreed that this leaves the cows with the *same* amount of grass, one of the houses is shifted to the corner of its field. As soon as this is done, he is certain that the cow feeding there now has *more* grass. Other children fail when there are two houses apiece, yet others with three apiece, and so on. If an attempt is made to prove to a child that equal spaces remain over, by showing him how two like sets of small cubes will exactly cover the two green areas left, he has his own answer. Though he had seen for himself that the two sets of cubes exactly matched each other, he now considers that the cubes, too, are no longer the same number.

At stage 2b (6–7 years) children have the right idea, but begin to waver if the visual contrast becomes too great.

At stage 3 (7–8 years) they are quite sure of their ground and will point out that there is the same number of houses in each case. If the questions are continued, they regard this as a joke. Or they may themselves remark that the amount of grass left looks different, but must be equal in each field, because an equal number of houses has been put in each.

4. THE NOTIONS OF LINEAR AND CIRCULAR ORDER

(i) *Reproducing a linear order*

Children are shown a rod with 7 or 9 beads of different colours threaded on it. They are then asked to pick out a similar set from a larger number of beads in front of them, and to arrange these along another rod in the same colour order. Or there is a "clothes line" with 7 or 9 pieces of "washing" hanging from it, and they are given another on which to hang a similar set in the same order, again taken from a larger array.

(ii) *Turning a circular into a linear order*

Children are shown a circular necklace formed by 7–9 differently coloured beads and are asked to arrange another set in the same colour order along a straight rod.

(iii) *Reversing the order*

The children are invited to carry out the foregoing operations in the reverse order.

(iv) *Stacking in direct and reverse order*

The "washing" is to be taken off the two lines and stacked in two baskets. In one case the child is to start at the left hand end, in the other at the right hand end, and whilst he is doing this, he is asked to say whether he can foresee what is going to follow what.

(v) *Reproducing a figure of eight*

Children are invited to copy a set of beads disposed in a figure of eight, either on a flexible wire which can be bent into the same figure, or on a rigid rod.

At stage 1a (3–3½ years) children can pick out the right colours or items, but have no idea of order. At stage 1b (3½–4 years) *pairs* begin to appear, at first only after a little prompting, but later also spontaneously.

At stage 2a (4½–6 years) children can reproduce the direct order, provided they can keep comparing and can put each bead, etc. under the corresponding one in the model. If this is shifted to one side, they fail. The circular and reverse orders are beyond their scope. The relation "between" is not understood yet.

At stage 2b (5–6 years) the direct order can be reproduced without the help of visual correspondence, and circular order can be translated into linear; but no reverse order can be constructed yet.

After an intermediate phase of trial and error, the child reaches stage 3 (6½–7½ years) where he can construct an inverse order by direct reversible thinking, without needing to grope or feel his way. The figure of eight or a widely spaced series may still present a little difficulty, but this is very quickly mastered.

5. THE NOTION OF ORDER
AS APPLIED TO MOVING BODIES

Three beads or dolls, A–B–C, joined together, are passed through a cardboard tunnel. The questions put are (i) in what order will they come out at the other end, (ii) if they go back through the tunnel, in what order will they come out then.

(iii) The child is made to sit on the other side of the table and asked the first question again. (iv) The beads or dolls having again entered the tunnel (in the original order A–B–C), this is then turned through 180° in front of the child, who has to say in what order they will now come out, at the same point. (v) The same question is put after *two* turns of 180°. (vi) The experimenter keeps on making these turns, first an odd and then an even number of times, and repeats his question each time. (vii) If a child has never claimed of his own accord that the middle object B would come out first, the tunnel is given a random number of 180° turns and he is invited to say which he thinks might come out first, A or B or C? If he replies "B" he is asked how this could happen. (The beads or dolls will only just go into the tunnel, so that B clearly cannot be pushed over the top of A or C.)

The above questions may also be put about 4 or 5 objects, and not merely three.

At stage 1 (4–5½ years) children can only answer (i) correctly. They assume that the reverse order will be the same as the direct, and even when the opposite is shown to them, they are unable to "learn" this fact in the sense of thereafter foreseeing it. In some instances, moreover, they may make the middle object come out first, even though they have previously seen that B cannot move out of its "in-between" position.

At stage 2a (5½–7½ years) they succeed with the straight reversal (ii) but with nothing more, anyway to begin with. At 2b (almost the same age-range) children manage (iii) and (iv) without difficulty, but have to fall back on trial and error for (v) and (vi). By this time, if there are only the three beads or dolls, the child can see that B must stay in the middle; but if there are five, he is still apt to suppose that perhaps one of those in between might come out first.

At stage 3 (6½–7½ years) the children straightaway give all the right answers for the right reasons.

6. THE NOTION OF DISTANCES TRAVELLED

The children are offered a board on which two lengths of string mark out two "tramway tracks". One forms a straight line, the other turns right and left in equal rectangular segments, and they start and end in alignment with one another.

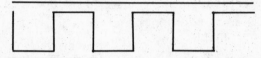

A bead representing a tram passes along each route. The experimenter's "tram" travels along several of the rectangular segments and he invites the children to make their "trams" go an equally long way along the straight track. If a child lets his "tram" stop exactly opposite the experimenter's, he suggests their going back to the station together, that is, the child's "tram" keeping level with his on the straight track, while he goes back segment by segment. This will mean that the child gets back first, and he can then be asked how this could happen. He is also offered a cardboard strip and told that perhaps he could use it to see whether the two tracks really are the same length.

At stage 1a (5½–6 years) children go entirely by the points of arrival. If these are in line, the same distance has been covered, and no proofs to the contrary can move them away from this belief. At stage 1b (5½–6½ years) judicious questions, and also what happens on the return journey, can bring the child round to the right view for a short time, but if the experiment is continued, he will tend to return to his first idea.

At stage 2a (5½–7½ years) he begins as in stage 1 but, helped by the discussion, he presently succeeds in detaching the notion of distances travelled from that of points of arrival. At 2b (6–7 years) he attends from the start to the actual lengths of the two routes, but is unable yet to do any measuring; the strip offered to him is rejected or disregarded, or else only applied in a random way.

At stage 3 (7–8½ years) he goes on to actual measurement, at first with some fumbling, later with full assurance.

7. THE NOTION OF SPEED

(i) *The speed of two movements where only their end-points are seen*

Two dolls are passed through two straight tunnels, one 55 cm., the other 40 cm. long. They leave and arrive at the same moment, and the child is asked whether one of them went faster than the other. If he fails with this, he is shown what happens, without the tunnels, so that he can see one of the dolls going faster than the other. The tunnel performance is then repeated and the same question is put to him again.

At stage 1 (5–6 years) the child insists that the two dolls went equally fast because they arrived together, and nothing can persuade him otherwise. Even though he has watched one moving faster than the other outside the tunnel, this, when no longer seen, is overruled by simultaneous arrival, which he *translates* into "moving equally fast".

At stage 2 (around 6 years) the child begins with the same idea but gradually works up to the right conclusion.

At stage 3 (6½–7½ years) the time and space relations are all *reasoned* out correctly right away.

(ii) *Fully visible movements, with common starting-points*

1. The children have before them a drawing of a straight horizontal road AB and another, AC, which diverges from this. They can see that AC is longer than AB and are told that two cars will be starting along them at the same time and going equally fast. Will one arrive before the other? Later on they are shown what happens and asked why the car going along AC arrived at C *after* the other had reached B. (2) The same questions are based on a straight and a winding road going from A to B. (3) The two cars travelling along

AB and AC now leave A together and arrive at the same time, one at B and the other at C. Has one gone faster than the other? What happens is then actually shown and the children are again asked to say whether the speeds were the same or different. (4) A similar sequence of questions is put about cars leaving together along the two roads, one straight, one winding, leading from A to B.

At stage 1 (5–6 years) the children expect the two cars, in the case of both (1) and (2), to arrive at the same time. When shown that one arrives earlier they insist that it went quicker, though they had been told that the cars were travelling equally fast. In cases (3) and (4), if the cars arrive at the same time, they must be moving at the same speed, even when the contrary has just been shown. Occasionally, however, a child will say in case (4) that the car along the straight road went faster because it was a shorter road. All the contradictory facts are explained away on grounds such as one car having been pushed, or not having gone fast enough, or both having gone very slowly. Neither the idea of speed, nor that of time taken, nor that of true distance, have been mastered yet. Greater speed means overtaking; if there is no overtaking, speeds cannot be compared, or else are the same.

At stage 2a ($5\frac{1}{2}$–$7\frac{1}{2}$ years) there is success with (1) and (2); the time taken is now seen to go with the lengths of the two roads, which no longer depend on the coincidence or alignment of their end-points. In (3) and (4), however, involving speed proper, the children fail, even after they have watched the actual facts. At stage 2b ($6\frac{1}{2}$–$7\frac{1}{2}$ years) there is a gradual realization of the right answers to (3) and (4), but only after the true facts have been demonstrated.

At stage 3 (7–8 years) the three ideas of length of road, length of time and speed are from the outset correctly related and structured.

8. THE NOTION OF TIME: SUCCESSION, DURATION AND SIMULTANEITY

A race is played out on a table by means of two small dolls which are made to advance at different speeds and by separate spurts along parallel tracks. The following questions are then put:

(i) Doll No. 1 goes from A to D, whilst doll No. 2 goes from A to B, and No. 1 then stops, whilst No. 2 goes from B to C. The child who has watched this is asked which stopped first. Or No. 1 is supposed to stop at midday, and the question takes the form: did No. 2 stop before or after midday?

(ii) Did No. 1 and No. 2 run the same length of time, or as long as each other, or if not, which went on a longer time?

(iii) If No. 1 stops at C and No. 2 *simultaneously* at B, the child is asked whether they stopped at the same moment or not, and if not, which stopped first.

These questions can be readily varied, e.g. different departure times, but simultaneous halts, or different starting points, but simultaneous halts at the same place, etc.

At stage 1 (4½–5 years) none of the time relations are yet distinguished from the spatial ones: "a longer time" means "farther"; "first" or "sooner" means "in front of" or sometimes "behind". There is no strict simultaneity, and duration is proportional to distance travelled. The child may consider that No. 1 took a longer time than No. 2 *because* it moved faster, or that No. 2 stopped sooner *because* it did not go so far. There are continual contradictions and changes of mind. Correct replies occur side by side with wrong ones and many of the answers appear just random.

At stage 2a (5–6½ years) time order and space order are beginning to separate out, though still very imperfectly. There may be progress with the idea of succession, but not with that of duration; or vice versa. Neither simultaneity nor coinciding durations may be grasped yet, or only one but not the other. At stage 2b (6½–7½ years) succession and duration are brought into relation and, with some help from the experimenter, the child gets his first proper hold both on the idea of simultaneity and on that of coinciding durations. However, a return to the old confusions may still occur.

At stage 3 (7–8½ years) time and space are at length fully sorted out. Succession in time is now clearly distinguished from spatial order, and co-ordinated with duration and with simultaneity in a single, reversible system. The child can deduce the correct reply to each question directly from this coherent scheme of time-relations in his mind.

V

EDUCATIONAL BEARINGS OF PIAGET'S WORK

1. WE SHOULD NOTE first of all that whilst Piaget's studies of the earliest years cover the whole basic pattern of learning, later he deals almost solely with *structural* growth, the framework concepts of space, time, number, and so on. We must thus distinguish between the more general bearings of his psychology as a whole, and what his *structural* enquiries imply for the specific education of children in arithmetic, geometry and related fields. There is of course no inconsistency between the two; the latter are a special case of the former. Both merit our most careful attention; the first for educational theory and practice at large, the second for some of its most troublesome applications. Both will be briefly reviewed below; but before doing this, we must clear out of the way a double misunderstanding of Piaget's findings, which often hinders their true assessment.

On the one hand his results have been taken to refer to the processes of native growth, or inward *maturation,* of the child's mind. On the other hand, they have been held to establish—or to claim to establish—the actual *age* to which each stage of this maturation is tied. Thus, on such an interpretation, children of 4–5 would be incapable of the idea of number, or of most spatial ideas, or of certain elementary logical ones, etc. Those of about 6 would only just be able to grope their way forward in very easy cases. One would, in fact, have to wait till about 7–8 before one could expect any real grasp of even apparently simple numerical, spatial, temporal or logical relations. This then, if valid, seems to call for drastic re-thinking of much of the work of all our ordinary Infant Schools; but it seems to set a barrier also to what the most "active" and progressive methods can do for children under 7–8.

However, as already said, all this is but a misunderstanding, even if it has been fostered at times by some of Piaget's own ways of presenting his results. Careful consideration of his work as a whole shows how mistaken is such a reading. First, as regards the relation of age and stage Piaget claims nothing more than that the ranges he cites represent his actual findings on the Genevan school-children who were tested. We find in fact that the ranges given are very wide, besides being mere averages. Furthermore, his detailed figures plainly show a large *overlap* between the stages. Thus some 4–5 year olds produce replies characteristic of the 7–8 average, and some 7–8's respond like average 4–5's. Piaget has himself insisted that his age-ranges are no more than a useful framework of reference for the way in which the stages *succeed* one another; it is the order of succession that matters, and not any particular chronological age.

On the other point, the apparent heavy stress on maturation, the answer is simply that what Piaget is setting out to study is not the differences which different environments might make, but the *common* stages and laws of *all* children's mental growth. There is enough scope in such a study to keep any investigator fully engaged without his going outside that task. This does not, however, mean *denying* the influence of outward factors, or treating mental growth as resulting only from inward maturation. On the contrary, Piaget's whole psychology rests on the principle of continuous *interaction* between the child and the world around him; it is this that furnishes all the material, as well as the motive force, for his intellectual advance. Thus there can be no question for Piaget of any purely internal process of development irrespective of the quality of the environment.

He would hold, of course, like most of us, that the way our human minds grow is at bottom prescribed by our human endowment and capacities, so that if growth goes on at all, it must assume certain characteristic forms. It is these in which he is most interested and on which he concentrates. But on his own premises one would expect that favourable or unfavourable outward conditions would bear strongly on the success and extent of development. The former might go far to promote it; the latter to arrest or warp it. Piaget would certainly have the utmost sympathy with any enquiry that aimed at establishing the *optimum* setting for mental growth. He might indeed well consider that his own findings pointed to what that setting should be, even though it was not for him as a psychologist, but rather for teachers, to work out the practical implications.

These implications do not in fact diminish the teacher's powers and responsibilities in any way, nor do they in the least support any attitude of just waiting whilst the child inwardly matures. The *order* of stages in mental growth is what Piaget is concerned to make clear; but whether they will be passed through with greater or less speed or zest or all-round gain, or whether the later stages will be reached at all, is a wide-open question. From that angle, it may be vitally important whether the educator has or has not provided the right conditions and help for the child.

2. This brings us directly to the light thrown on these conditions by Piaget's own new psychological picture of intellectual growth. Here we can first of all say broadly that what his psychology does is to supply a solid new foundation and a fresh weight and authority for just those pregnant insights which we already owe to the great educational reformers of the past. That of course becomes very clear, once the false

"maturational" interpretation is corrected, but the actual elements of this new accession of strength to "active" education merit a special glance.

(i) First and foremost, Piaget brings out all the *psychological* gulf between the true learning that is growth and the so-called learning which is mere verbal training, habit formation, or the mechanical mastery of skills and knacks. The former is our great human achievement, which starts practically from birth and in some degree goes on all our lives. Its main motor throughout is the child's own active doing, and learning from doing. Above all else, it is *cumulative*. That is, it forms a structure in the child's mind which he himself keeps building up. Each new level is only made possible by what has been built before, but then leads on to a further advance, and a greater and richer whole. The second kind of learning, on the other hand, has real value only as far as it provides *working means and tools* for the first type. If treated as an end in itself (whatever show it may make) it becomes worthless. Verbal "learning" can be "taught" by drilling and cramming at any time, but tends to be shed almost as soon as the cramming stops. Moreover, if it remains merely verbal, it is only a meaningless "act", even while it lasts. To *some* extent, of course, it can join up under favourable conditions with the "real" learning that goes on all the time, and to that extent it achieves true value; but how little that amounts to among average school-children is only too lamentably plain.

(ii) True learning is learning not only by doing but also by understanding. That however again means *genuine* understanding, which is intimately linked with doing and largely dependent upon this. As already emphasized, the child constructs in his mind in his first 18 months a basic working model of the world which he can then use for the assimilation of all his new experiences. That assimilation to what he already firmly holds is what brings the sense of understanding to him.

In the course of these further assimilations the original

model is itself constantly extended and further filled in. At the same time its content is being sorted and grouped and *ordered* in diverse ways, by various kinds of likenesses and relationships. Furthermore, as "accommodation" operates, and shortcomings and errors come to light, the model gets revised and, where necessary, re-organized. Thus if the conditions are right, it should steadily grow more comprehensive and better adapted to the real world, and this in turn should make it capable of ever more effective assimilation of new experience. Such assimilation can then more and more truly be called *integration;* that is, integration into an already existing organic scheme.

In this way growth should of its own momentum lead to further growth. It will be seen how essential here is *continuity* of doing and experience. *All the way through, further integration can only be built on effective past integration.* To the extent to which the wrong kind of learning (that is, learning without doing and experiencing, without understanding and integration) intrudes into the process, continuity is broken. Thus the very power of future integration, and so of future true learning, is in some degree impaired.

(iii) We have noted how, after the first framework has been constructed and language mastered, the child spends the next three years or so in vigorously enacting his further education by exploration and experimentation, by imaginative play and expressive activities, by talk, questioning and listening. Thus he discovers new experiences, incessantly works over past ones, compares, reflects, corrects, connects, etc., etc., and by the age of 4–5 has performed miracles of real learning. Therefore planned education, when it formally starts at around 5, has but to carry on what is being so successfully achieved already. Its special contribution can only be to provide such conditions and such aid that the same great educational work can be done *better still*. All its planning must be aimed at this one thing. The child's interests are to be stimulated further, his questions encouraged, and new problems, opportunities and materials put his way. He is to find help wherever he needs it, and active leadership that constantly carries him forward. The teacher's object should be to open up for him more and more paths by which both his present understanding and his powers of future integration can continue to *grow*.

If we now compare planned education in this sense with the traditional scheme of "school" as the place where children were trained in being taught, or learning "lessons", we can see how close that came to the very negation of growth. *All* its characteristic features: the buildings, classrooms, classes, enforced attention, and notions of "learning", were like a conspiracy to insulate children from everything that could help them to grow; and a conspiracy which for many was only too successful. The processes of living learning still went on to some extent outside school; but too often on a rapidly diminishing scale. Since for one thing school and "lessons" took up most of the available time, children's own growth tended to dwindle and fade away. More than this, the child's very *standards* usually suffered severe damage, because school lessons under school conditions came to be what "learning" and "education" meant for him. With the aid of the great educational reformers, we have gone some way towards changing this, anyhow in the earlier school years; but how far have we succeeded yet in getting all the underlying *wrong assumptions* out of our system?

(iv) Summing up the task of education as a Piagetian psychologist would see it, we may repeat that it must above all enable the child to carry much further what he is strongly impelled to do in any case. He urgently needs to try and build up in his mind a model of his surrounding world which will allow him to *foresee* at least its main course, to be prepared for it and to move and plan freely within it. We must help him both to get this model much better organized, and also to expand it, as far as lies in him, in some of the chief directions that radiate out all round him. Some lead to what we call geography, some to history, some to the world of living things; others to the different forms and sources of energy, or to elementary particles, or to the stars; and still others to the world of human and social affairs, institutions, thoughts, feelings and imaginings. Stimuli are always acting both *on* the child and *in* him to draw him in all these directions; in the end he must decide which draw him most, but to begin with, he can become curious and interested about virtually any of them. That is the most precious first asset of the educational process. These interests should be so fostered that his world will continually enlarge all round him, whilst yet remaining one world. Such it is in very truth; education need not create or "teach" this, but only has to ensure that it is preserved. All the child's natural learning by doing, experiencing and assimilating tends that way and makes it easy to help him, however widely and variously his vision may expand. On the other hand, we can also plan to break up his "one world", and the best recipe for this is undoubtedly to force on him all the discontinuities, the separate subjects and the taught "lessons", of conventional schooling.

3. If we pass on now to our second theme, the educational bearings of Piaget's work on the growth of *structural* thinking from 4–5 years onward, this from our current "school" angle is mainly a matter of arithmetic and elementary measurement and geometry. One chief point that has become clear is that the child's mental growth in these two fields is very much of a piece, so that they need to be taken closely together. By the same token, however, there are other basic structural notions which tend to develop at the same time and on similar lines; perhaps we should also give educational attention to these, in a way we have hardly started considering yet. Something more will be said about this later on, but the first question is what Piaget's work has to offer in the field of number and space-relations.

(i) First of all, it supplies the fullest psychological confirmation for what we have already taken in and begun to practise. The child can only learn in the true sense by (a) starting from what he feels to be real problems, problems that he is interested in and *wants* to solve: (b) working on them himself and *trying* to solve them. It is not essential that he should discover them all for himself, though the more he does so, the better. There is nothing against their being raised by the teacher—as, in the case of arithmetic and measurement, they may often have to be—so long as they spring naturally out of present concrete situations and are *actively taken over by the children*. Moreover, the latter need not get very far with their own attempts at solutions provided they are "engaged" enough to make a real effort. The teacher must in fact know *when* to come in with help (usually just by some pointer towards the next step forward); not so soon that children have not had a chance to make their own contribution, nor so late that they have become discouraged and bored. Most teachers, once this aim is clear to them, can usually feel their way to the right point of intervention. In any case if they are dealing with a group, the whole enquiry is a *joint* enterprise which they are merely leading and in which all take a hand, where they can or will. Thus the children themselves will fill each other's gaps and re-stimulate one another, yet will also find individual chances of relaxing, whilst the enterprise as a whole goes ahead.

(ii) Secondly, the important things to be mastered are not the rules for getting results right—which can too easily be a mere drill effect—but the *concepts* of number, of measurement, of length and breadth and height, of areas and perimeters, etc., so that each child can understand the problem. That means getting into his mind the hang of how we arrive at numbers, or at our elementary spatial concepts, how we can join them up and what we can do with them. Most children do in fact succeed in this, usually as early as 7–8, but it seems to come to them less through teaching than through the pressures of real life, which often confront them with the simpler number and space relations and demand some rudimentary *understanding* of these. It might, however, come sooner and more easily and might develop much further, if most of our laborious and unmeaning school lessons were replaced by activities in which the children themselves wanted to find out something. The material would not only have to be concrete, but interesting to them, and the problems such that if they could not think of the answers, they would be eager to know how one *could* solve problems like that. Here Piaget's actual experimental situations, as set out in his books on Number and Space, might well prove to be highly suggestive. They are all concrete and meaningful to the child; beads to be strung into necklaces, flowers and vases to be matched to one another, sweets to be divided up between morning and afternoon, laundry to be hung up in a certain order on a line; or challenging problems about building on an island, or planning a road, or placing players in a game, etc., etc. At the same time, however, all the situations involve numerical or spatial relationships that *test* whether children have the basic idea or not.

Of course, if they are completely unready for this idea like most of Piaget's 4–5 year olds, nothing can help. If, however, we look at the illuminating middle stage, a year or so on, where children are just beginning to grope towards the right solutions, we can watch how the learning steps start. Piaget records detailed discussions with some of them in which we can see how they progress, partly because they now feel puzzled by the errors and contradictions they get into, and want to find the right answers, and partly because the experimenter helps them on in various ways by questions that are hints or by creating suggestive situations. All this material richly repays study and is likely to indicate to any teacher countless further variations, both to meet the special needs of different children and to enable them all to grasp more readily the common principle, the master-idea, which is involved.

(iii) Here, however, a cautionary comment may not be out of place. It is not difficult to imagine enthusiasts hitting on the bright idea of turning the Piagetian situations to ordinary "teaching" account—or even of devising formal "play" materials based on the right relations, which the child would thus automatically be led to "learn". Clearly this might then just turn once more into mere meaningless learning-by-training. It might indeed well prove a more effective method than most past ones, and might lead to improved "results". But that would still fail to be real learning. This, as we have seen, depends upon children being able to integrate further elements into schemes in their minds which are integrated already and into which the new elements naturally and continuously *fit*. No formal material will do that, nor any situations taken out of their context for instruction's sake. Nothing will serve but what can be made meaningful to the child: that is, by being joined up with what is meaningful to him already; real felt problems, and also real felt *discoveries* about the way to solve them.

Accordingly, the Piagetian test situations can only help true education if they are made to come so alive that children will identify themselves with the problems raised by them. It may then happen that some pupils will get genuinely interested in the structural relations concerned and may wish to follow these up and to find out more about them. That indeed is the one satisfactory way in which a transition can be achieved, at least in a number of children, to real readiness for arithmetic and elementary geometry as such. Quite generally, the more successful active education is, the more strongly it should carry pupils over eventually to a true "subject" interest in various fields; and so to eager "subject" learning, which can then in turn become fruitful because it is genuinely integrated into their mental growth.

(iv) A word now about the other basic structural notions which Piaget has studied: movement and speed; time; physical quantities; and logical relations (like those of class inclusion or serial order, which all of us, *including children,* draw upon in our everyday reasonings). These enter only in passing into ordinary infant-school life, and several of them not by name at all. But when occasion offers, most of these ideas are *used*, however loosely, even among 4–5 year olds; and, as Piaget has demonstrated, by the age of about 7–8 the average child has achieved a good functional hold on them, at least in the easier cases. Thus he may be able to *handle* correctly notions like that of distance—rate of movement or speed—events succeeding one another or being simultaneous or overlapping—the logical relations between wider and narrower classes—and so on. If Piaget is right, these notions (always in their *"use"* aspect, not their verbal one) develop in fact at about the same time as those of number and space, because they are closely related and make up a single structure. Moreover, most of them are just as important for our practical lives as those of arithmetic or elementary geometry. Perhaps, therefore, if we think the latter worth so much attention, we might also devote some to those other ideas. Here, too, many suitable situations are set out for us in Piaget's books, and would stand at least as good a chance of holding children's interest as any "number" problem.

There are yet other basic structural ideas with which Piaget has not dealt so far, or anyway not fully. That applies, for example, to the vital notion of *causality*. This was the theme of one of his early books, written prior to his more searching techniques. It comes into his later experimental study of the first 18 months; but he has not as yet followed it through, by the same methods, from 4–5 years onward. As however the work on the first 18 months shows, this notion is even at that time one main support of the child's model of his world. And indeed it plays so controlling a part in all his subsequent thought 'and action that it seems to merit as much educational help as his ideas of number and space. It would in fact be specially rewarding for later *integrative* development. This, however, is too large and uncharted a theme for more than passing mention. More generally, the Piagetian type of genetic-psychological approach is itself still in midgrowth, and some of its most significant educational applications may yet be to come.

However, over against the foregoing suggestions, a final qualifying word seems desirable. It has been emphasized that the various concepts here called "structural" form the *framework* for the world-model in our minds. The *filling in* of this framework is supplied by all the child's concrete activities and experiences: his learning about land, sea, air and sky, about inanimate and animate things, about humans of every kind and their affairs, and so on. The structural frame is important, but what it holds is even more so. We may still be placing too much stress on the first, above all in its more formal aspects, at the inevitable cost of the second. Therefore, even though we may need to give attention to a much wider *range* of structural ideas than we normally do, this ought to be at the expense of other formal activities, like our laborious arithmetical drill, and not of more vital things. Framework and content should develop together, each in turn helping on the other; but framework pursuits must not, in early education, become too specialized or formalized. What matters from a broad human point of view is always the child's grasp of the basic *idea,* rather than his repertory of detailed performance. The value of Piaget's work is that in each field it lays bare the structure of those basic ideas, and thus allows us to focus our educational thinking on essentials, instead of our past inessentials. Yet they are still only *framework* essentials, and must leave scope for the child's fullest filling in. Here more than ever the principle of learning by wide and varied *doing, understanding* and *integrating,* must govern our educational plans.

BIBLIOGRAPHY*

| Evelyn Lawrence,
T. R. Theakston,
N. Isaacs | *Some Aspects of Piaget's Work* | National Froebel
Foundation,
1955 |
| E. A. Peel | *The Pupil's Thinking* | Oldbourne Press |

Jean Piaget	*The Psychology of Intelligence* *The Origin of Intelligence in the Child* *The Child's Construction of Reality*	Routledge and Kegan Paul
	Play, Dreams and Imitation in Childhood	Heinemann
	The Child's Conception of Number	Routledge and Kegan Paul
(with Inhelder)	*The Child's Conception of Space*	
(with Inhelder and Szeminska)	*The Child's Conception of Geometry*	

* See also publisher's bibliography, p. 119.

NEW LIGHT ON CHILDREN'S IDEAS OF NUMBER

INTRODUCTION

DURING THE LAST FEW DECADES there has been a radical new approach to the problem of what number means for young children—an approach supported by a large body of most interesting and revealing experiment. Furthermore this forms part of a far wider plan of research, covering all the child's most basic ways of learning and providing the most valuable new insight into his mental growth as a whole. I propose here to give a broad sketch of this new approach to number which we owe to Professor Piaget, but in a way which will, I hope, convey also something of its much wider background.

Perhaps two purely personal anecdotes may help me to strike the right keynote. The first might be called "Getting the knack of Arithmetic".

As a small boy I took quite kindly to counting and elementary number ideas; but at some time in my first few school years I started falling behind. I remember vividly puzzling my head about the *reasons* for what we were being taught, and being unable to see them; but it did not seem to occur to the teacher to stop and explain, so my mind just stayed blank and bewildered, and I failed to do my sums. It worried me to be unable to keep up with the other boys, and all the more because I liked figures; but there I was. Then one day came the blinding flash of the obvious. It suddenly occurred to me that perhaps one could *learn the rules* for doing sums without stopping to understand them first. Perhaps that was what the other boys, or anyway some of them, did. I tried this out and it worked like magic. I was soon holding my own with most

of the others, and after that, in the matter of arithmetical performance, I never looked back. But I recall that for some
time a haunting sense of having *cheated* remained.

My second anecdote might perhaps bear the title: "What
does number mean to the adult?" It may also help to illustrate, in a very contemporary setting, that the other boys may
not in fact have understood any better than myself what this
number business was really about. I found myself recently
discussing with a Training College lecturer in the teaching of
science the large theme of introducing some first scientific
ideas into junior education. Presently something led to the
not unusual question how far, for that purpose, mathematics
was a science. What exactly was in fact its status or relation
to the experimental sciences, or, if one liked, to all the other
sciences? My lecturer friend thereupon tentatively defined
mathematics as the making of certain assumptions and the
working out of their consequences. That seemed right
enough as far as it went, but obviously was only half a statement. I wanted to get a clear view of the other half which, it
seemed, was bound to be in my friend's mind, so I asked
him, "What assumptions, or assumptions about what?" His
sole answer was: "Ah, that's philosophy." There the discussion ended. That is, without more than a statement that by itself meant strictly nothing. In fact just half a thought, which
cried out logically for the missing other half.

Of course it is quite true that this way philosophy and its
unending argument lies. And speaking for myself, I have
spent so much time and effort on the argument with such
small satisfaction that I could certainly not criticise anyone
for shying away from it. But there does seem to be something
wrong if a teacher of teachers of science can rest content with
a formula which, *as it stands,* is not so much debatable as just
meaningless. Perhaps, on that question of what number really means he, along with most of us, has not after all advanced so very much further than we earlier youngsters did
—or anyway not further than from a knack-learning to a for-
mula-learning stage?

But now, from this anecdotage, let me plunge into my real theme. I have long thought that there could possibly be an alternative, or third course, out of our past dilemma of either having to balk on some illogical threshold of philosophy, or else being swept right over into it. Might not the science of psychology be able to throw a measure of *factual* light on the question of how we arrive at the idea of number—what it means for us—how we build up its rules—and on what its extraordinary potency and usefulness rests? But the trouble was that until a few years ago it seemed impossible to point to any psychological work of which one could say: "Ah, that is what was needed. That is what we had been waiting for." And this fact seemed to give support to the philosophers, who mostly poured scorn on the very idea that a mere empirical science like psychology could have any real light to throw on the idea or meaning of number.

Now, however, the situation has, I believe, radically changed. Professor Piaget's work has come along and in my view does fill the bill. It shows that when the approach and planning are right, the natural science of psychology *can* offer the most illuminating light firstly on the development of the idea of number in young children, and secondly on its relation to the growth of the child's mental capacities as a whole. And this then, since it gives us the way in which we ourselves came by the notion of number, yields us a new insight into its make-up and working in our own minds. So that, if teaching is our job, we can now hope to teach arithmetic with understanding, and can perhaps even aspire to teach the understanding of arithmetic. We need not suppose that Professor Piaget's labours, or those of any psychologist, can solve any ultimate philosophic problems. And even from a more modest angle some of his conclusions no doubt remain controversial. But he does provide at least a comprehensive working model, resting on facts and capable of being further tested, which we can follow through as far as it will take us. And that, I believe, is vastly further than anyone has taken us before.

That then is the basis for this invitation to plunge into a not too familiar or easy terrain. I shall try to offer a fairly careful survey of the main gist of Professor Piaget's volume, *The Child's Conception of Number*, which fully sets out both his theoretical conclusions on this theme and the experimental work on which they rest. But I should say at once that Number by no means exhausts the scope of this book. Whilst it is primarily a study of the first building up in the minds of children of 4–7 years of the idea of number—as distinct from the earlier mere knack of counting and the later mere knack of school arithmetic—it also aims at a much larger target. It links up numerical thinking with *logical* thinking in the widest sense, and seeks to show that their development is most closely related and indeed each depends on the other. The basic unity of mathematics and logic has been the theme of many mathematical philosophers and logicians for some decades. But Piaget has, I believe, been the first to turn this theme into practical experimental psychology, with direct bearings on the mental growth, and so the education, of the young child. In the present study my chief topic is intended to be number, and the new understanding and possibly the new methods in the teaching of arithmetic, to which Piaget's work might lead. However I shall also try to bring out something of the link-up with logic, which may perhaps add an extra touch of novelty and even provocativeness to the discussion.

I propose to begin with a thumbnail sketch of Piaget and his labours as a whole, with a brief note on their present scientific status. Then, setting out from our common assumptions about number and arithmetic, I shall seek to show in broad general terms how his findings impinge on these. After that will follow a summary of some of Piaget's main experiments and their results, together with a short discussion of the latter. Finally, I shall offer some few comments on the chief educational implications of Piaget's results, anyway as I see them.

I

PIAGET AND HIS WORK
AS A WHOLE

1. THE MAN AND HIS WRITINGS

FIRST OF ALL, then, Piaget himself. He is a French-Swiss genetic psychologist, born in 1896. He started with a training in
biology, and still carries this with him, but he soon became
more and more interested first in the philosophy and then in
the psychology of knowledge, which in fact became his main
lifework. For he had come to see in genetic psychology the
key to the growth of the human capacity for knowledge and
understanding as such. This meant for him, in essence, the
growth of logical, mathematical and scientific thinking, and
everything to which they have led. And by the age of 25 or
so, he had worked out a great plan of experimental enquiry
into the processes of intellectual development in children
from their beginnings to maturity. Together with a large
team of collaborators and pupils, he has been realising this
plan ever since.

From the early 1920's onward he published a series of
volumes on the language and thought of children, their judgment and reasoning, their ideas of causality and their notion
of the physical world. These were followed by an illuminating excursion into the development of moral judgment in
the child. Then came an intensive study of his own three in-
fants from birth onward, recorded in two remarkable volumes: *The Origin of Intelligence in the Child*, and *The Child's
Construction of Reality*. After that he poured forth studies of

Play, Dreams and Imitation in Childhood; of the growth of the notions of number, physical quantity, space, time, movement and speed; of the development of the child's logic and capacity for abstract thought, etc., etc. As his findings took full theoretical shape, he also published some more general works on the psychology of intelligence and on logic, and furthermore a three-volume treatise called *An Introduction to Genetic Epistemology*, which is a comprehensive analysis of the development of the main type of knowledge in both the race and the individual. A number of his books have not been translated yet, or anyway have not yet appeared in translation. Unfortunately also much of Piaget's work is at best not too easy to read, whether in the original or in its English rendering, and in one or two cases the latter has not served its author too well.

I should add here that in the opinion of some of us the first group of writings, though very stimulating, was open to deep-reaching criticisms. However, Piaget subsequently modified his procedure partly in the light of these criticisms, but still more of his intensive study of his own children and of all he learnt from them; and his later results in my view carry substantial conviction. The book on Number belongs to this later period. It was first published in French in 1941; the English translation came out in 1952. It is only fair to say that whilst the latter shows Professor Piaget as sole author, the French original joins with him a colleague, Mlle. Alina Szeminska, whose name should equally have appeared in the translation. However, it remains true that the theoretical inspiration was obviously Piaget's, as part of his total research plan, which had already gone on for many years. And he had always mobilised the labours of a considerable number of helpers, above all experimental; that in fact is one of the important sources of strength of his work. Their contributions have thus been material and should not by any means be underrated. (One of them, Mlle. Inhelder, is now a permanent close colleague who speaks with an authority second only to

Piaget's own.) Yet the master-plan remains his and he stays the true architect of the great structure of new knowledge and insight linked with his name. I shall therefore continue, if only for simplicity's sake, to refer solely to him.

2. HIS OVERALL VIEW OF MENTAL DEVELOPMENT: ACTION AS THE KEY EVEN TO MATHEMATICAL AND LOGICAL THOUGHT

If now we look at his work as a whole, the first point to note is that we have here a vast series of ingenious and searching experiments, spread over more than a generation and over most major aspects of intellectual development, all leading to mutually supporting results. The general viewpoint which Piaget formulated at an early stage has in fact, in the further course of his labours, been steadily confirmed, elaborated more fully, and again confirmed.

The essence of that view is this. The starting-point and crux of the child's intellectual growth is not—as it was long the fashion to assume—sensory perception or anything else passively impressed on him from outside, but *his own action*. And action in the most literal, physical sense of the term. From the beginning it is patterns of active behaviour that govern his life. Through these he takes in ever new experiences which become worked into his action-patterns and continually help to expand their range and scope. It is through actively turning to look or listen, through following and repeating, through exploring by touch and handling and manipulating, through striving to walk and talk, through dramatic play and the mastery of every sort of new activity and skill, that he goes on all the time both enlarging his world and organising it. His own physical activity thus enters from the outset into his whole world-scheme and indeed fashions it, supports it and provides the master-key to it.

In effect thought itself is now simply an internal version or development of outward action. It is action which becomes *progressively* internalised through the child's acquisition of language and his growing use of imagination and representation. It then goes on expanding under the guidance partly of social life, partly of the physical world, till it culminates in a great organised scheme of mental *operations*. This is governed by certain rules of *mobile* equilibrium that allow us to make the most flexible use of our knowledge and to regulate our thought-life to our utmost adaptive advantage. These rules form themselves into two closely related patterns, intimately interacting with one another and probably at bottom one, which we call logic and mathematics respectively. Their operation represents our intelligence at its most effective level. They can both be clearly seen at work in those great notion-systems whereby we order all our experience: space—time—objects—causality, and so on. Piaget traces the development of each of these systems from its beginnings until it becomes fully operational. And the key all the way, up to the *most abstruse forms of logical and mathematical thought,* remains *action.* The child stays an organism or person continually interacting with his environment and striving by ever more complex procedures partly to fit himself into his world, partly to fit it to himself, physically and socially.

So condensed a sketch may not convey overmuch at the present stage; but it is only intended as a first backcloth and I hope will gather further meaning as we go along. I should only make clear again that I am not putting Piaget's work forward as *fully* established but rather as a point of view which is tremendously worth following through, at least as a working hypothesis. And since over most of its range it has strong experimental support, we should either have to find some major flaw in this, or else be ready to treat it as something with which we must come to terms.

I should add here, regarding the view taken of Piaget's work by contemporary British psychologists, that it is still somewhat early days for any definite summing-up. Only within the last few years has widespread attention been brought to bear on this work, and active scientific research focused on it. There had previously been a tendency to treat it as interesting, but rather off the main line of advance of modern psychology. It was criticised as too philosophic or not sufficiently scientific, not properly standardised and controlled, not satisfactorily presented and badly lacking in any statistical foundation, etc. Some of the latter criticism is not to be gainsaid, as I shall note. However, in spite of all this, the sheer calibre and weight of the steadily mounting work has more recently begun to win through. In a number of places experimental psychologists have seriously started checking up on Piaget's findings, repeating this or that part of his investigations, organising closely related researches, and so on. Much of this work is still uncompleted, or unreported, or anyway unpublished. However, it can be said that several broad confirmations of his results, both as regards number and in other fields, have already been obtained. One particularly interesting instance is an enquiry recently carried through at Aden on the number-ideas of local schoolchildren representing the most diverse races, where the investigator was fascinated to obtain from Arab and Somali children just the same kind of responses as Piaget has reported on his European, that is Genevan subjects.

The broad confirmations found do not exclude points of difference, and it may well emerge that both his concrete findings and his theory need some qualification, above all in the direction of greater flexibility. On the other hand there is still much misconception about the meaning and effect of some of his views. Once this is corrected, I think one can fairly sum up that such confirmation as has already accrued, together with the cumulative and cross-checking force of Piaget's own evidence, has now established his work as a development of major importance that demands the closest attention.

II

PIAGET ON NUMBER—VERSUS OUR COMMON ASSUMPTIONS

1. OUR COMMON ASSUMPTIONS: COUNTING AS THE SOURCE OF NUMBER AND OF ARITHMETIC

COMING BACK to the book on Number, we can see now how close this is to the heart of his general theory. For it is directly concerned with both mathematics and logic, and with the child's first efforts to enter into these two basic ways of organising his thought. But before I turn to the perspectives which Piaget opens up, let me try first to formulate what most of us would ordinarily tend to believe about the meaning of number and arithmetic. We can then clearly assess just where his contribution comes in.

Supposing we start in the time-honoured way from a dictionary definition which, if it is nothing else, is at least an express attempt to formulate what we all *think* we mean. The *Concise Oxford Dictionary* gives as one of the basic senses of the word "number" the following: "Tale, count, sum, company or aggregate of persons or things or abstract units" and also "symbol or figure representing such aggregate". That certainly covers what most of us would regard as the important arithmetical sense. I imagine however that we should at once want to pick out the counting element and put the main stress on it. We should think of number as the result of any process of putting together one by one. We might then add that arithmetic begins when each successive term of a counting operation, from "one" onward, is represented by a written symbol forming part of a regular scheme by which all such terms can be represented. A number thus is, for a start, any member of a systematic counting scheme which begins from one and proceeds one by one; and it is *the* number of all sets or collections that can be formed by the same process carried to the same point.

This of course deals only with the natural whole numbers and does not pretend to be anything like a final, word-perfect definition. It can, however, pass, I hope, as a first attempt to refine out with a little care just what we do mean by number, in the arithmetical sense. And it does lead straight on to the further stages of counting in groups, instead of one by one; combining groups and separating them; combining sets of groups and dividing them; and generally moving backward and forward with complete freedom within our systematic scheme and working out the rules of all the different operations we can perform within it, whilst maintaining its *basic* character of one-by-one countability. The sum of these operational rules within that scheme would then be what, at least to begin with, we mean by arithmetic.

The basic pattern is thus very simple and counting may well appear all the open sesame the child needs, anyway for his initial entry into the field. When he has learnt to count he has, it seems, the main secret of number as such. The rest after that is just following through and elaborating, but above all doing the necessary grind. That is, learning the names of the larger numbers, learning the scheme for symbolising and arranging them, learning the rules for manipulating more and more complicated models and throughout all this, practice, practice, practice. Nowadays of course we realise the need for a broad basis of concrete number *experience,* and also for keeping our number-work in touch with the practical things that interest the child. Thus we help him to see the countless ways in which numerical problems constantly arise; the indispensable need for arithmetic in practical life; and its vast potency and value for successfully coping with the most varied tasks. In other words, we have more and more come to recognise that the child must somehow be *interested,* and must be kept interested, as the stages of the grind proceed.

But we also know full well that these are only stages on the way to real arithmetic. It is not in fact such until it has been *freed* from these concrete entanglements and distractions and turned into the science or skill of pure calculation based on pure numbers. It only becomes applicable, as it should be, to virtually everything, when it is in fact applied to nothing, and thus becomes true arithmetic and no other thing besides. However, we are likewise aware that the nearer we approach to this goal, the more liable we are to lose our hold on many of those we are trying to guide there. The further we penetrate into real arithmetic, the more we come up against children who dejectedly feel that they are no good at figures, or frankly detest them, or are bored or frightened by them. Many of these then only go on because they have no choice; but they do so on stay-in strike lines, and shed the burden the first moment they can, and if possible for the rest of their lives.

2. ARITHMETIC AS AN EDUCATIONAL PROBLEM: WHAT LIGHT DOES PIAGET THROW ON THIS?

In all this there seems so far to be no particular mystery or *theoretical* difficulty. We might reasonably conclude that numbers are a special interest or even a special gift, and that by and large we must accept the frequent lack, or low level, of this interest or gift as we find it. Since arithmetic is so essential a tool for most of the practical purposes of life we must somehow go on coaxing our young people into some minimal ability to handle it, by whatever ingenuity or skill we can muster. We must ease and lighten the grind and employ whatever adventitious aids we can devise. And above all, we must, as already stated, strive to enlist and maintain their interest. Even so, it all remains, with too many of our children, a very uphill business and even among those teachers who have in the main accepted modern ways, some may perhaps, in this matter of figures, look back with a little nostalgia to earlier days. That is, to the days when children were expected to make every *effort* to learn, however uninterested, what *we* knew they would need, and if they dragged their feet, could have salutary pressure applied to them. And of course many teachers still think this the only possible way, certainly with figures, if not with everything else.

The pity of it is however that for so many small children counting, when first learnt, is fun, but arithmetic is not. Yet the latter could be all the *games* one can play with counting. But that does not get through to the child. For him arithmetic is something quite different, namely just the grind of "sums"!

What light now does Piaget's work throw on this situation? Can he help us to understand better what happens in our children? Can he enable us so to handle the transition from counting to arithmetic that the latter will remain *alive* for the child? And how does he view the relation of the two, and indeed the nature of arithmetic? Here we may find ourselves plunging into somewhat deep waters. But let us turn now to what Piaget actually tells us.

III

THE OUTCOME OF THE EXPERIMENTS

1. GULF BETWEEN CHILD'S ABILITY TO COUNT, AND THE "IDEA" OF NUMBER

THE FIRST and most startling thing which Piaget demonstrates is the great gulf there is for the young child between being able to count and even the most rudimentary real numerical idea. Counting for him does not generate number. It is an enjoyable minor skill which he readily learns up to let us say "ten" or even higher, and then goes on performing for its own fun's sake. But he may not have any glimmering that a number, once counted, has any existence or status of its own, or is equal to another number similarly counted, or that it cannot grow or shrink by turns, or even do both at the same time.

And there is no reason to think that these are things he learns through the arithmetic he does at school. He does move on to them, often within a matter of a few months, but this may well happen before his school arithmetic has begun. Children down to 5 years may already be in possession of true number ideas. But older ones, however assiduously "taught", may not have them yet.

What must actually take place, as Piaget's work shows, is an inward course of growth, a process of organisation and structuring, as a result of which an idea that did not exist before is presently found functioning and in clear control. The child now *behaves* quite differently from the way he did before. What had completely baffled him a few months earlier has become self-evident and a matter of course. Contradictions and absurdities at which he had not turned a hair, he now dismisses with adult scorn.

That does not mean—as we shall see—that this inward process goes on irrespective of what happens to him in the outer world. School arithmetic may not have much to do with it, but that is another question. The important point for the moment is that whatever may or may not happen from outside, there is a great *psychological* distance to be spanned between the child's learning to perform counts, however proficiently, and his attaining the first genuine, working idea of number in his mind. Piaget demonstrates this by first evidencing in a dozen different ways the complete *absence* of any such idea at the initial stage of his experiments, and then in the same dozen different ways its full *presence* in children who are some months or perhaps up to a year older. Thus from the ability to perform counts to the possession of the idea of number a spanning process does and must occur within the child's mind. At his half-way stage, in the same dozen different situations, Piaget shows the process actually happening.

What is particularly interesting, of course, is the manner in which, by this progressive experimental analysis, he brings out all that enters into the make-up of the genuine idea of number when it *is* there—in the child or *in us*. Counting remains the final key, but it is the key to a far more complex psychic structure than my earlier account of our ordinary assumptions might have suggested. What the bearing of this may be on the problem of education in arithmetic is a separate issue. The first need is to acknowledge the facts and to try to understand them. The complex psychic structure which we designate as the proper idea of number may, as I have already noted, be present even in a 5 year old. But it is vital to realise that it is present only as a functioning structure, not as an explicit concept, and the child is quite incapable of giving an account of it in language, as Piaget has done for *us*. That indeed is likely to remain true for the rest of his career, and for that of most of us, even if we become the most expert arithmeticians, or possibly even mathematicians. The trouble is perhaps precisely that this functioning psychic structure gets formed so early and then goes on functioning *so automatically and unawarely*. Thus may be created the great psychological gap between the child's first achievement of the idea of number and what seems to so many children the dead and meaningless grind of their school arithmetic. Perhaps the value of Piaget may be to enable the teacher, with a new understanding of the child and even of himself, really to cope with this gap. But of that more later. Let me only acknowledge here for myself that Piaget's way of taking the idea of number to pieces and reassembling it, and better still showing us how it gets put together in the first place, has made the concept come far more *alive*, as well as far more clearly articulated, in my own mind than it ever was before.

2. NUMBERS AS "PERSISTING" PRODUCTS OF COUNTS, AND MEMBERS OF A REALM OF NUMBERS

To return to the child's own unsuspected long voyage from the mastery of counting to the idea of number, the crucial fact is that, in the initial phase, his interest lies in the activity, not in its product. The latter, the resulting number, is just not conserved as such. Counting signifies not numbers but *merely* counts. If the child is challenged or tested on numbers as such, even when he has just generated them himself by counting, we find that they have dissolved immediately into a general blur, in which they are fused with size, shape, spacing and their perceived context generally, and it is one or another of these directly perceived elements that dominates, whilst the counting as such counts for nothing.

What must evolve gradually instead is that the product of the count somehow begins to persist for the child, as itself an object for attention and interest and, as it were, now an entity existing in its own right. It must remain linked with the count and controlled by this alone; but different countings should engender in the child's mind the idea of a whole realm of such count-generated entities; and gradually an ordered realm, all of the same kind, in which one can pass from one member to another and eventually from any member to any other, by regulated repetitions of the same counting activity.

This realm must thereupon be more and more completely separated—always in the child's mind—from the context of perception, from size and shape and spacing and arrangement and all their changes and vicissitudes. It must be turned into the notion of a world apart, which, in contrast to perception, is up to a point entirely under one's own control. In that world indeed one can generate numbers just by one's own counting, even if one has nothing tangible to count, or anyway nothing but tokens or imaginary units. But one's control is now merely that of the points of entry into this world. As the child begins to attend to the numbers he has counted up as members of *their* own world, he comes to see that they have their own nature and properties, all linked up with one another. And thus counting becomes for him merely the way into this special realm, which one must study and learn about, just as with the physical world. He will then be ready to find that there is a subject, a school-subject, arithmetic, which consists in just that learning. But by that time he will probably have lost the original and controlling link with counting; this will be a very elementary activity which for most purposes he has left behind; and the world of numbers and arithmetic as such will most often seem a very dead and boring one, which means nothing whatever to him.

That is something like the cycle through which too many of us pass. If, through one cause or another, we do stay interested, we can recover eventually the counting-key by which the whole world of number is formed and controlled. And if we turn to Piaget we shall find that for his theory this does indeed remain the master-key linked up with his whole view of human action, operation and mental development.

3. SURPRISING NATURE OF PIAGET'S FINDINGS

Thus the wheel comes full circle and Piaget shows how and why it does so. At the stage of the small child, however, all that concerns us is that before he can *handle* even the most elementary number-situations, he must first form a properly structured idea, or functioning schema, of number and numbers. And for this purpose he must somehow get the order or system of number, as a separate self-existing realm controllable only by counting, into his own system.

How utterly remote he is initially from this, we shall see from the behaviour of Piaget's first stage children in his actual experimental situations. Most readers are completely taken by surprise by the extent of the failures, the contradictions and absurdities, the blank incomprehensions, into which Piaget's youngest group, however much at home in counting, appear to fall. Many people are indeed strongly inclined to discount the experimental reports and to question the validity of work that seems to lead to such incredible results. They suggest that the questions are badly put or misleading, and that anyway the children have obviously failed to understand them, or else cannot express their answers properly. After all, as they say, in stage 1, these infants are for the most part only 4–5 years old. But this sort of negative attitude cannot really be sustained in the face of all the detailed discussions with so many individual children, the diversity of experiments and the changes rung on each one, and the various forms of concrete help given by the experimenters. Furthermore, as I have suggested, the case is most strongly clinched by the evidence of a half-way stage in which the children can be *seen* feeling out towards something they have not quite reached yet, scoring partial successes in easy cases, now advancing tentatively and gropingly, and now falling back. And so that no one can say that the grasp of number which is being tested is far above the heads of small children anyway, we have already noted the further fact that at an average age of only a year or so more, there is the most complete antithesis to the first-stage picture—a set of answers by children of 6–8 years as rational and adequate as an ordinary adult's, and as *confident* as his could possibly be.

Thus the very surprise and incredulity aroused by Piaget's first-stage results is a measure of the novelty, the value and revealingness of his work. The great gulf between counting-ability and even the most rudimentary working grasp of number is both proved to be there, and proved to be success-fully bridged. The process by which the small child does so is in truth one of internal growth—for what else could it be? But, as I have indicated, we must be on our guard against jumping to the conclusion of so many readers of Piaget that he must mean a *purely* inward growth or maturation; that is, one which takes place quite independently of the child's out-ward life. That does not follow in the least. Piaget's own in-terest lies in laying bare the nature of the total inward evolu-tion of the child's mind, and he does not concern himself with outward circumstances. But when occasion arises he does expressly acknowledge the effect they could have on the detailed rate of different children's mental growth. And above all one should remember that his very model of such growth turns on the child's active relations with the world around him, and his continual interchange with this through his action upon it and its reaction on him. His basic pattern of advance is continuous varied activity bringing the child further and further experience, and then the embodiment or assimilation of this in his action-patterns which in just that way expand into ever wider scope and richness. That is no model of purely inward or maturational growth. It may on the contrary entail an educational approach for which only the self-education pivoted on the child's own activities and active experiencing is psychologically real. That would be very much more in line with Piaget's own educational sympathies and outlook. But this is a theme to which I must return in my final discussion.

IV

THE PRESENTATION OF
THE EXPERIMENTS—AND
THE EXPERIMENTS THEMSELVES

1. DIFFICULTIES AND STUMBLING BLOCKS

I COME NOW at length to the actual tenor of Piaget's work on Number and his detailed experiments. I have spent much time on the theoretical build-up, since without it most of the value of Piaget's findings must inevitably get lost. In fact the book itself is distinctly difficult to read, and even more so to consider and appraise. I naturally do not wish to discourage anyone from trying it; my object, on the contrary, is to praise Caesar, not to bury him. But one must be well-warned for a somewhat laborious enterprise, for which the author himself does not afford overmuch help. And just because nevertheless it *is* so important and enlightening, I feel I must add some more cautionary comments before I pass on to the detailed comments of the book.

(1) Most of the theoretical part—as distinct from the experimental material—is written in an abstract and often highly technical vocabulary which Piaget does little to explain. Thus he draws freely on the language of modern, formal logic, and also rather seems to assume that his readers will be already familiar with his own theoretical thought. One can still follow most of his thought, even if one is not equipped in either of these ways; but the going is undoubtedly hard.

(2) He fails to give reasonable introductory information

about the actual place and circumstances of his tests, or even about the numbers of children tested. I *believe* the work was done partly at a nursery school in Geneva with which Piaget had long been associated, and partly at Genevan infant and primary schools. The children were not sorted out in any way as regards intelligence level, and no particulars in this respect are provided.

(3) Piaget exhibits his results, as already indicated, in terms of three stages: a first one showing the total lack of any idea of number—a second or intermediate one which exhibits some groping and uncertain progress—and a third one where normal adult-level responses are produced as a matter of course. But these are not in the main three stages in the growth of the *same children*. There are a few cases where the same child does crop up again, a stage further on. By and large, however, the subjects are mostly different, not only for each experiment, but for each stage. All that really happens is that Piaget cites, in each instance, some total-flop responses, some half-way ones, and some that are confident and correct. These he marshals as his three stages. The only direct link with the observable facts of individual growth is that the average ages of the children in each successive group show a *progressive increase* of a year or so.

This emerges in spite of much overlap, with stage 3 responses from some children in their 6th year and stage 1 reactions from some between 7 and 8. That of course is just what one would expect from unselected mixed groups, in which some 5 year olds might have a mental age in advance of that of other children aged 7. Probably the progression would have come out far more sharply and impressively if mental ages had been determined and these instead of chronological ages had been correlated with the stages. Also people would not be misled into linking particular stages with particular chronological ages, and either trying to refute Piaget by challenging these linkages, or else drawing quite unwarranted educational conclusions from them.

On the other hand one would have liked to know more about the children of about 7 years who were still in the total-blank stage. They, and the slow movers generally, might well provide a large proportion of those who later on could not get on with figures—perhaps *because* they never had the right active experiences for the vital first step. But these are speculations in which one gets little aid from the way the data are presented, or perhaps have been collected.

All one can say on the whole theme is that Piaget seems to rely mainly on the *internal evidence* of progression between his three stages and although such reasoning *could* be dangerous, in fact his evidence seems to me extremely convincing. Moreover the advance of each stage in average age does provide noteworthy extra support. I might perhaps add that the number of children whose similar and surprising total-flop responses are given is 77—quite a respectable figure.

(4) The actual sequence of experiments, though in the main logical enough in the light of Piaget's own theoretical thought, seems to entail one or two anomalies even by this standard. In any case, however, it presents additional stumbling blocks to those not familiar in advance with his thought. He starts from cardinal numbers, but oddly enough *begins* with some experiments in *continuous* quantities, i.e. with liquids, which seem rather off his main target. Then he considers at great length ordinal numbers and their relation to cardinal. After that come some experiments in pure logic and much discussion of these. Finally there is a return to cardinal numbers in a more developed form, illuminated, as Piaget holds, by both the ordinal and the logical discussions. This progression involves some points of theory which I personally regard as controversial, but cannot try to cope with here. I shall chiefly focus on the cardinal number sections, which I think are what most of us have in mind in connection with arithmetic, and can only refer to the ordinal-number work in passing, but I do want to leave some little space for the vital and most suggestive cross-reference to logic.

Furthermore, I shall depart from Piaget's own arrangement in another way, but this time simply for the sake of properly bringing out what I myself found his most dramatic effect. Piaget, for each experiment, gives in sequence the "stage 1", "stage 2" and "stage 3" responses. I shall group together all the experiments on cardinal numbers and then present all the stage 1 responses, in order to demonstrate the full reality and consistency and unshakable non-comprehension of this stage. I shall then more briefly illustrate the stage 2 and stage 3 answers, and proceed in the same way as regards the logical experiments.

2. THE EXPERIMENTS AS PLAY SITUATIONS

With this I come to the experiments themselves. They are all put in the form of *play* situations into which the children generally seem to enter with interest and even zest and, up to near the limit of their capacity, with ready co-operation. I have no space here for the details of the "pretend" build-up, but great ingenuity as well as understanding of small children's ways has gone into devising most of the situations, so that they should come as naturally as possible to the children, anyway to begin with, and carry them along.—In the case of cardinal numbers one main way in which Piaget and his helpers tested whether any idea of number as such existed was to vary the shape, apparent size, spacing and arrangement of a group the children themselves had counted, and then to see whether they stood by their counted number or not. Another way was to try if they could do something as simple as matching a given counted group with another equal in number, either one by one or any way they liked. A third order of tests was whether they could re-arrange two unequal heaps into two equal ones, or appreciate something so elementary as that two equal sets of things, even if thereafter subdivided differently, would still stay equal. In other words, by all these tests, had the child really advanced from counting to the *idea* of a number? Could he think in terms of this, or *with* it, or *use* it as an idea? Did a number as a number have any meaning for him yet? Did he naturally turn to counting as a check on it? And where he counted one by one, had he any notion yet of a unit as a unit, of a number as made up of units, and of two equal numbers as made up of corresponding units?

With these questions well in mind, we can let the following brief summary of the actual sequence of cardinal number experiments and their results tell its own tale.

3. DESCRIPTION OF CHIEF "CARDINAL NUMBER" EXPERIMENTS

(1) Two equal lots of beads are counted out into two similar containers where they reach the same level, and the children see them to be equal in every way. One lot is then put into two differently shaped containers, first into a wide and shallow one, then into a tall and narrow one, and they are asked whether there is the same number of beads in the new vessel as in the untouched original one, whether it would make a necklace of the same length, etc.

A similar experiment was carried out with two quantities of liquid filling two exactly similar glasses to the same level and then poured into different shaped vessels, and also into two or more small ones.

(2) (*a*) The children are requested to match various sets of objects with another set which would naturally go with them: bottles with glasses, vases with flowers, egg-cups with eggs. Or to use a given number of coins to buy sweets at the rate of a sweet per coin. If the child manages this, the experimenter then spreads out or closes up one set or the other, so that they are no longer the same length, and puts the question each time: are they still the same number?

(*b*) Since the natural link between these sets might be providing non-numerical help, the children are given piles of

counters and simply asked to pick out from these the same
number as there is, first, in another lot put down anyhow,
then in a set pattern, then in various closed figures, simple or
more complicated, then in a row.

(3) (*a*) Two equal lots of sweets are arranged first as four
each to be eaten in the morning and afternoon of two days,
and then as four each to be eaten in the morning and afternoon of one day, but only one for the morning and seven for
the afternoon of the following day. The children are asked
whether they would be eating the same number each of the
two days.

(*b*) They are handed two unequal piles of counters and
asked to make them equal.

(*c*) They are supplied with a single pile and requested to
divide this up equally between two friends.

(4) (*a*) After they have seen a set of say 6 flowers matched
to 6 vases, and then the 6 vases matched to another set of 6
flowers, they are asked if they think the first set (of 6) is the
same number as the third; and also if two of the sets together
are two times the third.

(*b*) They are given various lots of liquids in different vessels with the query whether these are the same quantity or
different, whilst at the same time they are offered a glass and
other empty vessels to help them find out. The point then is
whether they will take in that they can use the glass as a unit
or measure, for comparing the quantities. And also whether
they will see that using the glass twice gives two times the
quantity, and using it three times gives three times the quantity. That is, how far the idea of *measure* and *units* means
anything to them.

4. TYPICAL FINDINGS: STAGE 1

Now in the case of every one of these experiments and every
variation of them there was a number of children, classified
by Piaget as at stage one, mostly 4–5 years old, but some

older, who proved hopelessly at sea. But there were others who could give the right replies where they were helped by perception or trial and error, though they went back to stage one as soon as appearances went against them, or anyway went badly against them. These, mostly 5–6 years old, but some younger as well as some older, represent Piaget's transitional stage 2. Finally a number, mostly 6–7 years old, showed that they really had the idea of what number means by giving the obvious answers, as child's play.

For the authentic flavour of the first stage, one must read Piaget's detailed account of the replies of each child to the succession of questions put to him. But I shall try to indicate at least their typical pattern.

(1) *First, the conservation experiments with beads and liquids*

Most of the stage 1 children thought that when one set of beads was put into a taller but narrower container, it became more because it reached higher. Some, however, held that there were more when they were put in the shallower but wider container, because they were spread wider. It did not even occur to them that the number would or could still be the same. And even if the beads were put back in the original container and once more seen to be the same, they became different again as soon as they were retransferred to the different shaped vessels. And this was *not* merely a question of getting mixed up between number and height: when a child was asked whether the numbers would be the same or different if the beads were poured out on to the table, the reply was that there would be more of those poured out of the taller glass, because they came *from* a taller glass. The replies were still the same even if the child himself put the beads one by one in turns into the two different containers; the taller one, or else the wider one, was still said to have more beads in it. When it was suggested to the children, in order to help them further, to imagine the beads being strung into a necklace, they pictured this out in detail but remained convinced that the beads from one of the containers would produce a longer necklace.

The pouring of a given quantity of liquid from one vessel to another yielded exactly parallel results. As an interesting variant, a child who had decided that there was more liquid in the taller vessel than in the original ones, was asked to mark the level which he thought each liquid would reach when poured into similar larger glasses. He indicated two very different levels and was greatly astonished when the pouring had been done and he saw they were the same. The child was so convinced that the quantity of liquid had become different that when he observed the same levels, he suggested that in the case of the original lower level glass, some liquid must have been *added*.

(2) *The matching experiments*

(*a*) First of all, the stage 1 children, who could to all appearance count, just could not match 6 glasses to 6 bottles, or 6 flowers to 6 vases, or 6 eggs to 6 egg cups. They set up some sort of a row and then floundered. One took 12 glasses, put them close together, thus got a shorter row than the 6 bottles and thereupon said there were more bottles than glasses. Another matched 7 glasses to 6 bottles and when shown by their being arranged one to one that there was a glass over, he asked for another bottle. When he had this, however, he put the bottle at the end of the row, so that he now had a bottle over at one end and a glass at the other, and said they were *not* the same number. A third child held that 6 bottles were less than 5 glasses because the latter made a longer row, but then brought the 5 glasses closer together to make them less, and so *equal* to 6 bottles. Another child had matched 4 eggs widely spread out to 7 egg cups, and manifested real surprise when he came to put the eggs inside the egg cups and found he had *not enough*. He then got hold of 12 eggs which he put close together to match the 7 egg cups, and was again very surprised when he came to put the eggs in the cups and found he had *too many*. Exactly the same type of result was obtained when the situation was repeated in terms of flowers and vases, or varied in terms of coins exchanged one by one for sweets. These contrasts between the ability to count, apparently like ourselves, and such utter failure to grasp what counting means and does are surely cumulative and astonishing. Employing it as a way of verifying a number, or of comparing two sets of things, or finding out if they are the same, just does not come into the children's minds.

(*b*) When asked to put out counters equal in number to a random group or a pattern, or a closed figure, or a row, they again behave in exactly the same way. They make a rough total guess, or they try to imitate the pattern or figure, and only succeed in getting the number right when the figure happens to be a simple and familiar one, such as a square with one in the middle. Counting again does not occur to them. In the case of the row, they try to match not its number but its length or closeness together. One child happens to get his number right, but his row comes out longer, so he says "that's not right", and takes some away. Another child puts 10 coins close together to match a row of 6 sweets, but even so the row of 10 is shorter, so he adds 2 more to make them the *same* number. Still another first matches 6 with 7, and says that the row of 7 is more because it is a longer row, but then corrects himself and says that the row of 6 is more because they are so close together. Once more, number is just not number yet, has nothing to do with counting, and is nothing more than "a-lotness" or "a-fewness", "moreness" or "lessness", according to one aspect or another of its *appearance*.

(3) *Splitting-up and equalising experiments*

(*a*) The stage 1 children (who in the two cases quoted are actually 5¾ years and 6 years 11 months respectively), do not begin to understand, and even with help and prompting cannot be got to understand, that 1 plus 7 sweets are the same as 4 plus 4, and that the total remains the same. Both children insist that they will be eating more sweets the second day, because seven is such a lot. They stick to this even when the sweets are shifted backward and forward between 4 plus 4 and 7 plus 1 in front of their eyes. Thus again, no trace of number as number yet, and no thought of counting.

(b) Children shown two unequal lots of 14 and 8 counters and asked to rearrange them so that they are both the same, shift them around haphazardly. One turns the 14:8 grouping first into 16:6, then into 7:15, then again 16:6, then 5:17. Another ends up with 13:9, and so on.

(c) Children asked to divide 18 counters between themselves and the experimenter, so that they each have the same, take a shot at splitting the heap into two equal lots, but simply by sight. A child chances to get two lots of 9 each, but one of them takes up more space. So he decides that he has gone wrong—and just shifts the two lots over bodily to take one another's place. Another very carefully and correctly distributes the original heap one by one between himself and the experimenter, but then decides he is wrong and the two lots are not the same, because one is spread more. A third child puts the counters one by one in separate boxes, and declares them equal, but when the two boxes are emptied out and one lot comes out closer together he considers it fewer.

(4) *Experiments to test the idea of numerical equality as such, that of unit or measure, and that of the simplest multiple relations, such as two times or three times*

(a) There is as usual a group which registers total failure. Out of two who have just put one red and one blue flower each in several vases, one is very *uncertain* whether the number of red and blue flowers is the same or not. The other is sure they are not, because one lot as set out takes up more space. In a variation of the experiment, a third child, who has "bought" successively the same number of blue and pink flowers for the same number of coins, denies that he has the same number of each because the pink ones came from a bigger heap of flowers held by the experimenter. When the pink and the blue flowers are each matched one to one with the pennies he says: "Ah yes, they are the same." But as soon as the separate buying begins again, he returns to his belief that there are more pink ones. In another variation a fourth child has put *two* lots of 10 flowers each in 10 vases. He is given some small flower-holders and shown that they will only take one flower each. He is then requested to take enough of these small holders for all the flowers. He thereupon gets hold of ten, which he places one to each vase. When the question is put whether he has enough for all the flowers, he takes another four. He is invited to try them out and towards the end adds another two, but the idea of two holders to each vase never dawns on him. A fifth child also starts with ten holders and then adds 5 or 6 more. A sixth one, who has made up two sets of 10 flowers to go with 10 vases, is asked: "If I want to put all these flowers into these vases, how many must I put in each vase?" He answers: "One." After trying this out on 5 or 6 he discovers he needs more and finds at length that he has put in two each. But this puzzles him and he enquires: "*Why* does one have to put in two?" He fails in the same way as the other children with the one-flower holders, of which he sets up 10 to take the 20 flowers. When he finds he has not enough, he adds first 4, then 3 and then another 3, and thus gets all the flowers placed; but once more he enquires *why* he needs more holders than vases. Only with still more help does he at last rise to the idea that two holders are needed for each vase.

(*b*) The experiments on the ideas of units or measures or simple multiples are completely above the heads of the lowest age-range group. The children get so far as to pour the liquids backward and forward, by way of showing their general sense of the problem, but they expect quite different levels for two equal amounts of liquid, can make nothing of their equal findings, entangle themselves in contradictions, suggest that merely pouring a quantity into another vessel makes it more, and generally have no glimmering of the relations involved.

5. typical findings: stages 2 and 3

So much for the stage 1 reactions, which are very much alike in all the experiments. Once more let me emphasize that since the children are for the most part not the same, all that can strictly be said is that for every experiment there is a number of children who behave in a certain way which Piaget calls pre-numerical or stage 1. Thus if we talk of stage 1 children producing those reactions, this is only shorthand for the fact that there are children who show that reaction, which we then classify as stage 1.

The same applies to stages 2 and 3. In each case there are children who give transitional responses and others who produce matured and perfectly correct ones. The former are grouped as stage 2, the latter as stage 3. Yet it is reasonable to *infer* on every sort of ground that in fact all children must start from what Piaget calls the first stage where no idea of number is present yet, and must pass through some sort of intermediate or half-way phase such as Piaget calls stage 2, before they can attain the level of the fully-formed idea of number, which Piaget designates as stage 3. Furthermore we can also legitimately conclude that each stage shows the general characteristics which emerge from the responses to the experiments and are taken up into Piaget's general developmental theory. Stage 2 is of course in the nature of the case much less clearly defined than either 1 or 3. There is every kind of intermediate performance between the wholly negative extreme of 1 and the wholly positive one of 3; Piaget himself cites some responses which he calls transitional between stage 1 and 2, or between stage 2 and 3. However, it is possible to place in relief something like a characteristic picture of the *midway* region between stages 1 and 3, and I shall now give a range of illustrations to bring this out. And in each case I shall go on briefly to stage 3, obvious though this is, simply to show how the story rounds itself off.

(1) *The conservation experiments with beads and liquids*

The stage 2 children dealing with the beads could get the necklace answer right, because they had only to think of length. They went wrong, however, about the different shaped containers, because they could not attend to height and breadth at the same time, but were overborne by the perceptual effect of one or the other. Similarly with the liquid poured from one vessel into smaller or different shaped ones. Here they could hold on to conservation in the case of transfer to two smaller glasses or to vessels not too greatly different in level or breadth, but fell down on three or more glasses or large differences in shape. Thus it is plain that they still had not really mastered the principle of the thing—though one or two pulled themselves up after having gone wrong and in the end produced a stage 3 solution.

Children fully in stage 3 give the right reply as a matter of course and say at once: "It's always the same thing." Or: "I saw it was the same thing." Or, in the case of the liquid: "We've only poured from one glass into another" or ". . . into some others." Or: "There seems to be less in this glass because it's wider, but it's the same thing." Or: "This is narrower, so we must fill it up more."

(2) *The matching experiments*

(*a*) Stage 2 children can do the actual matching of glasses to bottles, flowers to vases, and so on without difficulty, or anyway very soon after a first false start. But there is still no real notion of *numerical* equivalence or constancy: overall appearance still carries the day against counting, and after testifying to six bottles and six glasses because, as the child himself says, he has counted them, he succumbs to either wider spacing or serried closeness, and affirms more bottles than glasses or vice versa. Similarly with the flowers and vases, and the coins exchanged for sweets. The stage 3 children say boldly: "Nothing is changed, you've merely put the glasses closer together." Or: "Spreading makes no difference, because the flowers were in those vases." Or: "Same thing," and when asked why: "Because one can match."

(b) Putting out counters equal to a random group, a figure, or a row. In stage 2 the pattern is more or less correctly reproduced, and amended if necessary till the numbers do correspond. But if the original collection is then spread out or otherwise changed, the children cannot sustain the equivalence. In some cases, however, particularly in the relatively simple ones of the rows, the child himself restores his sense of equivalence by bringing the spacing back to exact correspondence. Stage 3 children break up the model, if complicated, for easier matching; or do not try to follow it at all but just count freely and place their own counters in a line; or when the experimenter alters the spacing of the rows, one of them comments: "It's the same thing; you've spread out one line and brought the other close."

(3) *Splitting up and equalising experiments*

The stage 2 children still tend to go wrong over the relation of 7 plus 1 to 4 plus 4, but themselves readily notice there is something amiss as they focus attention first on the 7 and then on the 1, with contradictory results. Finally they fully see the point. When asked to equalise two unequal groups, they try to turn them into two similar figures or patterns which they can then adjust by transfer till they exactly match. Similarly with the division of a collection into two equal quantities. But they do not just *count*, and change of spacing or arrangement or even of orientation of the figures, or if they themselves start with a too complicated one, soon throws them out. Stage 3 children explain precisely and at once why the seven plus one are the same as the four plus four, pointing to three out of the seven as accounting for there being only one left. They equalise the unequal quantities by forming a simple pattern or straight line, and matching. And they divide the collection equally by splitting it 1 by 1 or 2 by 2. In each case, moreover, nothing which the experimenter may say can move them off the equality they have established.

(4) *Experiments on equivalence of three or more groups, on units of measurement, and on simplest relations of two to one or three to one, or one to two or one to three*

Children in stage 2 in this set of experiments may already be quite firm about the equality of a given set of flowers and a set of vases, and also of another set of flowers and the same vases, but are still liable to prove very shaky about the equality of the two sets of flowers to one another, or may positively deny it. However, they themselves may then think of checking up by direct matching and so reach the correct conclusion, though only on rule-of-thumb grounds. Differences of spacing may upset this again, but the upset may be rectified by bringing the three sets into exact correspondence, and counting may be brought in to clinch the matter. In the experiments which involve matching two narrow flower holders against each vase to take *two* lots of 10 flowers each, the stage 2 children proceed by trial and error and eventually arrive at the correct solution. Similarly, in the experiments to test children's ability to use a unit measure to compare the equalities or inequalities of quantities of liquids in different shapes of vessels, those in stage 2 oscillate a great deal and contradict themselves, but tend to pour backward and forward experimentally and finally they do thus arrive at a somewhat sketchy form of the notion of using a given glass as a unit of comparison and measurement. They make also some attempt at co-ordination of level and width, but whilst they have the right idea, they are uncertain how to give effect to it. More generally, they start in tentative fashion to try and work things out by reasoning, on the basis of what they already know, but have no great confidence in this and usually decide that the only sound way of reaching the right conclusion is by practical trial and error.

The stage 3 children know exactly what they are about. The two sets of flowers in the 10 vases are the same number, because the child has counted the one set of 10 and he knows that the other matching set must also be 10 without even counting them. Or he says he saw what was in the vases, and then simply counts by these. Again, the children at once recognise that it needs two of the one-flower holders to each vase to hold the same number of flowers previously arranged two in a vase.—When it comes to measuring, one child answers that he thinks the quantities in two vessels are the same, but he will have to measure. He does so, and confirms his judgment. Another rightaway starts measuring, makes a slip, but immediately corrects himself.—In the further experiments involving simple proportions, the stage 3 children reason the answers out, and one adds that measuring would show the same thing.

6. EXPERIMENTS ON ORDINAL NUMBER IDEAS AND THEIR RELATION TO CARDINAL

This is a long and detailed section which, for reasons of space, I must unfortunately pass over very briefly. Piaget holds that the child's notion of ordinal number develops in the closest relation with his cardinal number ideas and in fact each depends on the growth of the other, in the same way as both inter-depend with the growth of the child's logic. He and his co-workers have carried out a sequence of highly ingenious and interesting experiments based, first, on ordinal numbers and series as such, and then on their relation to cardinals. The results are very closely parallel to those already described; there are the same typical responses of total failure—of some very imperfect and qualified successes, based on easy cases—and of instant, matter-of-course solutions, just like an adult's. These different levels of response are spread out in time, over approximately the same age-range, as for the cardinal experiments.*

I am not sure whether Piaget establishes in fact more than that children's understanding of ordinal numbers and relations depends on their developing grasp of cardinal ones. He, however, attaches considerable importance to his own view of reciprocal dependence, for the purposes of his theory of logico-mathematical development at large. I cannot pursue that issue here, beyond acknowledging that I do not find this part of his thesis wholly convincing and adding that it does not seem to me so very important for his standpoint as a whole. But in any case the experiments remain most interesting at the least as a further contribution to the total picture and additional confirmation of this.

7. EXPERIMENTS ON CHILDREN'S GRASP OF SIMPLE "LOGICAL" RELATIONS

We have here a chapter for which most ordinary readers would probably be least prepared in a work on the development of the child's conception of number. It comes moreover in the middle of the latter theme and as a vital part of the entire structure. However, we have already seen that this springs directly from Piaget's basic conception of the intimate relation of mathematics and logic and their joint controlling role throughout the process of human intellectual development. And such a conception leads inevitably to the question how the growth of the child's simplest notions of logical relations fits in with that of his elementary arithmeti-

* Those interested in a short account of these experiments may be referred to the brochure *Some Aspects of Piaget's Work*, obtainable from the National Froebel Foundation, 2 Manchester Square, London W.1. This contains, *inter alia*, a detailed résumé of the entire Number Volume, which follows Piaget's own order of presentation, and may in general be found useful as a supplement to the present study.

cal ideas. Accordingly Piaget takes the purely logical relation which comes closest to a numerical one, namely that of part to whole. This is exemplified by the typical and far-reaching relation of any sub-class or sub-classes to some wider class in which they are included, equivalent to the familiar logical antithesis of *some* and *all.* Piaget constructs a number of experimental situations involving that relation, to see how far young children have grasped it and can handle it.

Thus, for a start, he has a box containing wooden beads, mostly brown, but two *white,* and the children are asked: "Are there more wooden or more brown beads?" To make the question easier and more intelligible for 5–6 year olds, he tries to help them to picture it out by asking which would be longer, a necklace made from the wooden beads or one made from the brown ones? To assist them further, he provides two empty boxes beside the full one and enquires in succession: "If I take out the brown beads and put them in this empty box, will there be any left in the first box?" "And if I take out the wooden beads and put them in the other empty box, will there be any left in the first box?" Only when these questions have been correctly answered does he go on to this further one: "If I make a necklace with all the wooden beads there would be in *this* box, and another with all the brown beads there would be in *that* box, which would be longer?"

The problem is further varied by having all the beads the same colour, but different in shape; mostly square, but some round; or mostly cones, but some round. Or different in size; mostly large but some small. Or, again, it is made still more evident to the eye by having two sets of beads, so that the children can actually visualise the two alternatives at the same time. And furthermore Piaget tries varying the proportions and bringing them much closer together: instead of 18 brown and 2 white beads, he has 20 brown and 18 of another colour. Finally, he tests what difference it would make if instead of artificial classes he worked with natural ones, very familiar to the children: such as a quantity of flowers, of which most are poppies, but 2 or 3 cornflowers; or even children in a school-class, of which most are girls, but a few boys.

However, all these questions, down to their easiest forms, draw completely wrong answers from a number of children between 5 and 7 years. The only effect of the helping hand given in the various ways described is to shift the age range of failure down in the main to 5–6 years. The children who fail, i.e. who are at stage 1, insist, however hard they are pressed, that there are more of the bigger sub-class than of the total class; that the former would make a longer necklace; that there are more poppies than flowers; that there are more girls than children in the schoolroom, and so on. They may describe the wooden necklace as brown *and* white, or may do a drawing of the brown necklace, with all the beads filled in black, and of the wooden necklace, with most of them filled in black, but two left white. Nevertheless, they still declare firmly that the brown bead necklace will be longer than the wooden one. Similarly a child will himself say that if the brown beads are taken out of the full box, the white ones will remain, whilst if the wooden ones are taken out, nothing will remain, but will yet maintain that the brown necklace would be longer. One child even enquires whether only white beads will be used for the wooden necklace and, when answered "No," goes on to ask, "The brown also?" and herself says, "Yes, because they are also wooden." Nevertheless she still insists that the brown necklace will be the longer one.

Parallel results are obtained with all the other versions of the problem. In terms of 13 blue beads, of which 10 are shaped like small cones, and 3 are round, a child can say that there are more cones than blue beads because there are many cones; and when the experimenter asks, "But what about the blue beads?" the child can himself reply, "All are blue," whilst yet when the question is repeated whether there are more blue beads or cones, he affirms once again, "More cones." In other words, many is more than all. In terms of blue beads mostly square but some round, a child who is told that one little girl wants to make a necklace with the square beads and another girl with the blue ones, laughs and says of her own accord, "They're all blue." Nevertheless when she is called on to say which necklace would be longer, she states with conviction, "The one with square beads, because there are more."—In terms of the flower problem, a child who is asked what is left if the poppies are picked, can answer, "The cornflowers"; if the cornflowers are picked, then "The poppies"; and if the flowers are picked (after a pause for reflection): "Nothing." In spite of all this, however, when the experimenter again puts to him whether it is the poppies or the flowers that will make the bigger bunch the child replies: the poppies, because there are such a lot of them.

Thus Piaget once more establishes a stage 1 at which children of the age-range of 5–7 years have not yet *begun* to grasp the nature of the relation of a larger class to the subclasses included within it, or conversely. In other words the part can still be greater than the whole. This is true even if it is not in fact much larger than the remaining part, and thus does not stand out as the main bulk of the larger class; thus where out of 38 wooden beads, there were 20 brown and 18 green, there was still the same typical insistence on the part of various children that there were more brown beads than wooden ones.

Stage 2 children find their way to the correct answers, but only by intuitive groping, not by reasoning. They begin by going completely wrong, as at stage 1, but then stumble on what must strike them as a good judicial solution, though in fact no less incorrect. A typical child says at first that the brown necklace will be longer because there are more brown beads. He is then asked again: "Are there more wooden beads or more brown ones?" His answer is: "More brown. No, more wooden. No, *both the same!*" Actually three children tried this way out. Eventually, however, with more questioning, they correct themselves (unlike those in stage 1, however much they may be questioned and helped), bring in the other coloured beads, and give the right answer. Even in stage 3, two of the children quoted fell at the first moment into the old error, but quickly and completely rectified this. The two others cited gave the right reply at once and explained why.

In sum, then, Piaget finds that at about the same age at which children have not yet any grasp of even the simplest numerical relations they have equally little grasp of the simplest *logical* ones (in the distinctive sense of this term). He goes on to establish that as the child advances to stage 2 and then to stage 3 in respect of numerical grasp, so he also progresses in the strictly logical field. In these facts he finds confirmation for his view regarding the close kinship between arithmetical and strictly logical operations and their interrelated growth, and he goes on to show, by theoretical analysis, how near to one another they in fact are and how they can only develop together.

V

GENERAL DISCUSSION

1. PIAGET'S THEORY OF NUMBER, AND
ITS RELATION TO LOGIC

THE FOREGOING WILL, I think, have given body to the stages
by which, according to Piaget's findings, the child proceeds
from a first phase of counting ability but complete lack of the
idea of number to the final one of full functional mastery of
it.

I have tried to spare ordinary readers most of Piaget's
technical vocabulary about the addition of relations, the multiplication of relations, additive and multiplicative composi-
tion of relations and equalisation of differences, etc., etc. But
I think I should at least sketch the groundwork of the theory
of number which he puts forward and which he believes that
his experimental findings have firmly established.

As I have already indicated, this theory is intimately
bound up with his view of logic. He holds that number is a
synthesis or fusion of the two basic processes that underlie
logic: that of *classification* leading to hierarchies of wider and
wider classes, such as those of plants and animals, and indeed most other kinds of objects, processes, or situations;
and that of *seriation,* or arrangement in a graduated order,
which is applicable to most physical qualities and properties
and to a vast number of relations, as diverse as those of
space, succession, kinship, social rank, etc. Piaget's view, if I
understand it correctly, is that whilst classification is based
on *similarity* and seriation on *cumulative difference,* number is
a form of grouping that arises when these two types of order-

102

ing are brought together into a single operation which sheds something of each and fuses the rest. The class of natural whole numbers is a class of which the sub-classes are a series. In fact the class of such numbers is formed by a single process of cumulative seriation. If one takes 2, 5, 28, 103, they are the names of sub-classes of the class of numbers, as spaniels, terriers, bulldogs, and greyhounds are the names of sub-classes of the class of dogs, or gold, copper and cobalt are sub-classes of the class of metals. But the sub-classes of the class of numbers are linked with one another in a continuous series or ladder formed by the repetition of a single process of generating new members by the addition of a like further element. Quality and with it difference are completely eliminated; nothing but the process of seriation and class-formation by seriation remains.

Accordingly the whole scheme is best developed in terms of abstract symbols and in fact of a scheme of such symbols. Numbers are not things, like classes and sub-classes of natural objects; they are products of the mind resulting from a basic process of the mind elaborated into a *system*. Number as such is only grasped when it is seen as a progressive *system* of numbers built up by this process. But when once the system is given, we can set up rules of movement which allow us to move freely within it in all directions, composing and combining members in any order or any clustering, and decomposing or splitting these clusters or *reversing* any previous operation or set of operations *ad lib*.

This system, Piaget insists, has most of its characters and properties in common with the separate systems of classification and seriation which he regards as the groundwork of what he calls qualitative logic. There are some much-controverted questions involved here, but it does seem to me that at the least a striking parallel with logic, both in actual functioning and in psychological history, is brought out.

2. THE ODD EDUCATIONAL SITUATION
ABOUT LOGIC

That leads directly to a question to which I imagine few of us ordinarily give much thought, namely that of education in logic, or the teaching of logic as such. The situation here is really quite an odd one. We all agree that arithmetic is one of the great basic subjects which, at least in an elementary way, everyone must be taught. But why is not logic recognised as equally basic and equally needed as a part of every education? Is it really less vital to us than arithmetic throughout the course of our lives? We all have to *reason* as soundly as we can, all the time—in every problem or emergency of our practical life as well as throughout our social one. In particular we continually discuss with others, and they with us, and we with ourselves, courses of action as well as beliefs and views, and we all of us take it for granted that we can usually tell sound reasoning from unsound. We base the whole of our lives on inferences and beliefs which we consider cannot be wrong, and there is hardly a situation in which our safety and success does not depend on our capacity for thinking with at least some approach to logical validity.

There is thus an overwhelming case for holding that logic, as the theory or "subject" of the processes and rules of valid reasoning, should be taught as universally as the three R's. Indeed even reading and writing, to say nothing of arithmetic, would be little use to us if we could not back them up with some grasp of logic and the demands of sound reasoning or inference or argument. If that is so, however, why is logic as a subject hardly ever taught except to budding philosophers or theologians or, in limited measure, to a minority of scientists? The parallelism of the processes and rules of logic to those of arithmetic makes the anomaly of our totally different educational attitude towards them all the more striking.

Of course the answer is that we are so accustomed just to

take logic, as a functioning system, for granted. We assume in the main that we find it in ourselves, as it were by the light of nature, and do not have to learn or teach it; and that to some supplementary extent we pick up the finer points of it as we go along in the course of our earlier practical experience of mutual communication and social life. But why then does not the same apply, or why is it not left to happen, in the case of arithmetic?

The interesting light shed by Piaget on these unaccustomed questions is that to a large extent the same process *does* happen, and is left to happen, in arithmetic. The most central rules and principles of this are also not taught to us. Notions like those of conservation, composability, associativity, reversibility, which are the keys to the possession of the very idea of number, never enter into ordinary arithmetic teaching. Here, too, we assume that the roots are somehow present in us natively, and that up to a point the setting of our ordinary upbringing is enough to help them to sprout and grow. The child is taught in the nursery, and picks up as a game, the activity of counting, and that, together with the innate capacity of his mind, is held to set him up with the first elementary idea of number. But of course after that we behave in a way totally different from what we do, or rather fail to do, about logical thought. We realise full well that between the idea of number, which we postulate as soon as the activity of counting has been got going, and any sort of proficiency in arithmetic there is a long and arduous road which can only be travelled by much diligent learning and above all practising. What happens in the parallel case of logical thinking?

The further insight provided by Piaget here is that neither the idea of number nor that of logic are just found in ourselves in the way we tend to assume. Both involve complex processes of inward structural growth, and in his view the two processes of growth, as we have seen, are closely interlinked. Indeed under existing conditions that of logic is a much slower one; children master the basic functional idea of number at around seven, and secure their first clear ideas of the implications of class-inclusion relations, as Piaget shows, at about the same time. But for the ability to handle logical relations with the same freedom and matter-of-courseness with which they manipulate simple numerical ones from $6\frac{1}{2}$–7 years onward, we must wait, in the case of most average children, till they have reached the age of 11–14 years. Yet perhaps this has something to do with our very different educational attitude to the two subjects? I can only raise this question; it is too difficult and complicated to try and consider in detail here.

There are just two comments, however, which may be worth making. First, the working logic to which most of us are led by the supposed light of nature plus our social apprenticeship is hardly very perfect. It is not to be underrated: most people do develop quite a competent capacity for the appraisal even of abstract reasoning and argument, more particularly other people's and the spotting of fallacies, more particularly other people's. But how much room for improvement there might be!

Secondly, the old traditional logic of the syllogism is not something that most present-day logicians would want to teach, at any rate as their main theme, if their subject were suddenly adopted as a school target, on a par in importance with arithmetic. Nor is this the logic with which Piaget is most concerned and which he exhibits as growing in close correlation with arithmetic. It has taken logicians until the last few decades to discover that logic is, or ought to be, something altogether wider than the scheme we had inherited from Aristotle. For the modern relational point of view syllogistic reasoning is only a limited special case. Thus the problem of why logic is not taught as much as arithmetic could not really have been posed *in adequate terms* until our time; there was no logic to teach comparable in scope with arithmetic. And, in my view, it is only Piaget's work that has given real searchingness and importance to the problem, precisely because it has shown that what matters most is not verbally learning the rules and the unfamiliar polysyllabic terms, but the complex *functional* structure or organisation which has to be built up in our minds, both in the field of logic and in that of arithmetic. Thus the problem now is in effect quite a different one. What is it that really governs the inward building up of this structure, its rate and degree of progress? To what extent can the real inwardness of arithmetic be taught, any more than that of logic? And so we come to the threshold of the question: what are the educational bearings of Piaget's work?

VI

EDUCATIONAL BEARINGS
AND QUESTIONS

1. MISUNDERSTANDINGS TO WHICH
PIAGET'S WORK LENDS ITSELF

I HAVE ALREADY at various points partly forestalled this theme. But let me try now very briefly to pull the threads together.

(i) First of all, I hope I have largely removed the fundamental misconception to which Piaget's findings have given rise in the minds of many people. He brings out the great process of slow and complex inward growth, spread over the whole field of mental life and all the years from birth to the threshold of adolescence, by which our minds develop into their full functional capacities and organisation. The child's growth into his first functional grasp of the idea of number is one important part of this total process, though a comparatively early one. Many of those who have followed Piaget's work have tended to see this slow inward process in *antithesis* to the action from without of teaching and education. Thus it has seemed as if the latter's scope were being challenged and indeed radically limited by the boundaries now apparently set by the true reality within. What could be taught appeared to become something extraneous and superficial which was meaningful only if it followed in the wake of each stage of inward growth and merely exploited what each of these made possible.

With that tendency went a closely related one to take Piaget's stages and the chronological ages with which he linked them much too literally. The stages again were construed as something inward and almost organic which, if Piaget was right, had to be respected; and the age-ranges established by Piaget then seemed obviously the natural guide to them. Conversely, however, it also appeared as if Piaget could be refuted by attacking this supposed linkage, by showing that the claimed chronological relationship frequently did not hold, by criticising the supposed fixity of the stages, etc., etc.

(ii) I have already suggested that all this is in the main just a profound misunderstanding. It is not an unnatural one and Piaget himself has lent some colour to it, first, by his almost exclusive focus on the study and understanding of the *inward* processes of development and secondly by the manner of presentation of many of his results and even of his theories. One might go further and query the slant of some of the actual theory and I should myself want to alter its balance in some respects. By and large, however, the factor of sheer misunderstanding remains. Piaget's basic view of the very process of inward growth is, as I have pointed out, pivoted on the continual cycle of interchanges between the child and the outward world: his action on that world and its reaction on him. It is this cycle that is the very motor of the child's mental advance, which proceeds by a constant rhythm of in turn assimilating outward reality and accommodating to it, on an ever-widening and ever more effective and powerful scale. Thus outward reality is as all-important for inward growth as the inward impetus in the child himself. As regards the stages, all but the largest divisions are merely convenient ways of breaking up the continuum of growth. And even these must be so interpreted that they are compatible with that underlying continuity; they simply mark certain major rhythms in it: phases of relative consolidation and temporary stability whilst the ground is being prepared psychologically for the next surge forward. The chronological linkages are no more than an approximate method of marking out the *sequence* of the distinguishable phases of growth, the order in which they follow one another.

(iii) Thus in reality the scope of education is not in the least narrowed or threatened by Piaget's work. What becomes all-important is merely the way and the means by which we try to educate. Certainly outward teaching which is not related to inward growth, and to the stage which this has already reached, becomes peculiarly futile and meaningless —as meaningless as progressive educationists have long contended it to be. By the same token any approach which is not based on *clear and full understanding* of that growth must inevitably fail, even if the utmost will to educate from within is there.

But we can now also invoke a positive counterpart to all this. Piaget's work as a whole has made plain all the vital education that goes on in the child quite independently of the set educational processes, and above all in his first few years, before those processes have even begun. Indeed, by far the most important portion of his intellectual growth is achieved by himself, through the direct working of the interchange cycle by which he actively learns to take in all the main features and the general make-up of the physical and social world around him. In that way, though he starts from practically nothing but the familiar "blooming, buzzing confusion" of his first few weeks, there is formed in his mind, by the age of 5–6 years, a far-reaching *functional working model* of his surrounding world. And if we watch all he does and says and clearly understands, even for only a few average days in say his 6th year, and try to work out for ourselves, without any preconceptions, everything which this ordinary round of his performances, practical and intellectual, implies, we shall see how very much that model must be there and how far-reaching it must be. It is only, in effect, because he has this model constantly operating in his mind that he can play the natural, largely spontaneous and actively participant role in the world around him, which we normally take so much as a matter of course.

If that is a reasonably correct and significant picture, what is the scope left for any would-be *theory* of education, that is, theory of *planned* intervention in the child's life to put him in possession of at least the most important historic gains and achievements of the society round him, gains which otherwise he would probably miss, or at best attain much more slowly and imperfectly? Surely all the accent must now fall on putting him in *real* possession, not merely verbal and apparent? And real possession must signify, at the least, not less real than that of the working world-model he has built up for himself and can successfully draw upon for every sort of purpose and contingency of his life. In fact real possession can only mean incorporation into that world-model, thus continually *expanding* it to the point of *transformation,* in exactly the same way as it has been expanded, and transformed by expansion, up to the 5–6-year level. But that then requires that we as educators shall fully understand that process, as it has already happened and is still happening, in all the tremendous sweep of its achievement; and that we shall intervene in it only, as it were, *with* its own current, making use of all its momentum and aiming simply at guiding and helping it on. Its momentum, however, is a direct function of the child's own activity, his exploring, enquiring, forward pressing interests, his wish to extend his knowledge, to understand and to be able to do. These have already carried him incredibly far and can carry him immensely further, up to the true limit of his capacities.

Formal, mainly verbal, teaching, by subjects, as we normally envisage it, has its place in this process, but if it is not to produce mere patter, or the verbal semblance of knowledge and understanding instead of its reality, it must in most fields come in only slowly and relatively late, when the ground is fully prepared for it. In other words, when a broad and solid foundation of wide-ranging active experience actively worked over, and a strongly established, positive, forward-reaching and self-helping attitude, has already been built up. For only thus is the child or young adolescent enabled to meet deliberate subject-teaching half-way, or, still better, three-quarters of the way, with a true capacity to *understand;* which means, to transform verbal material into a real psychic structure in his own mind, and one which can become continuous with the real structure that is already there. (This of course does not exclude the recognition that even in the earlier years some teaching in the conventional sense is unavoidable, since there is much that *can* only be verbally learnt—that is, which is not significant in itself, but solely a means to significant ends, and can only be acquired by memorisation and practice. The one important point is merely that this sort of teaching or "learning" shall not be mistaken for true learning or education—or thrust on the child in place of the real thing, where anything significant is at stake.)

And thus Piaget's work brings us back to the insights and the methods and objectives which progressive educationists have long urged on us—the stress on understanding the laws of the child's true inward growth, and co-operating with these and using them to lead him on and guide him; the value placed on his own active interest and own active thought; and so on. But thanks to Piaget, there is now available a new massive body of actual psychological knowledge which most powerfully supports the vision of the great educational reformers, and at the same time can, we may hope, be drawn upon to realise that vision with a new efficacy and success.

2. POSSIBLE EDUCATIONAL USES OF HIS NUMBER STUDIES

What, in conclusion, can we say of the application of all the foregoing to the specific theme of number—and, if Piaget is right, by the same token to logic? Let me defer the latter for the moment and merely emphasise again that for Piaget the two themes are most intimately related. In fact they constitute for him the twin tools which, above all, the child has to learn to understand and master, in order that he may increasingly be able to organise and to extend, to enjoy and to exploit, all the experience and knowledge which his activities bring to him throughout his life and growth.

What then of number-learning, the practical business of arithmetic and arithmetic teaching, as such? Since I am not a teacher myself, I can only most tentatively venture into the field of practical applications, and must leave this in the main to others better equipped with experience and know-how than myself. A few broad conclusions, however, seem reasonably clear. First of all, in the most general terms, it does look as if there should be something that merits the attention of working teachers in the wealth of actual concrete situations devised by Piaget and his helpers, which so plainly bring out where children stand about number, from nowhere through to full (functional) grasp of the idea and its due working control. Thus these situations can be used, for a start, to *test* how far small children have advanced towards that idea; and we can make sure that they have attained it before we try to impose any formal arithmetical teaching or learning on them. Otherwise this will just leave their minds behind, and will almost inevitably go forward either as mere rule-memorising and knack-learning, or, too often, without even that effect, or any at all.

Secondly, the Piagetian situations actually show us, in terms of his stage 2, some of the typical steps by which children accomplish their advance from sheer helpless floundering to trial-and-error groping and then on from this to grasping the right idea. There is much in Piaget's own reports to indicate that such situations can be fruitfully used to help children on their way; in a recent check-up on his findings this was actually done. Moreover, it would be surprising if all these ingenious and novel, but yet so obvious experiments, if considered by imaginative working teachers, did not suggest endless further variations and developments of a similar kind.

The vital point, however, is the way in which Piaget permits us to see our arithmetic and mathematics—even as our logic—as of one piece with the rest of our intellectual life and growth. What thereupon emerges directly is the pivotal importance of ensuring that this intrinsic unity shall be *preserved* and not *severed* by our educational approach. It may *not* be preserved even if children "learn" their arithmetic successfully in terms of words and figures and get their answers to sums "right". It is not *necessarily* preserved even if they are taught their first arithmetic in terms of concrete objects and familiar practical interests and activities, from shopping onward. It is only preserved in so far as, first of all, children start by forming their own true inward structured idea of number; and secondly, but far more difficult, if the later rule-learning, operation-learning and so on, becomes a living graft on that idea, or rather, is successfully developed as a further stage of its own inward growth. Can we learn to carry most children with us, in full understanding and lively interest, as we equip them to expand the world of numbers progressively for themselves—and thus enable them to do so as an integral part of the total pattern of their growth, continuous with every other, and an organic segment of the whole? And after the initial effort has been made, is there perhaps a chance that this may actually in the long run prove easier than the dead weight of drudgery, lightened only by extraneous artifices, which until now we have kept on inflicting on our children and ourselves?

Whatever the answers to these widest questions, however, I trust that readers of this study will at least feel prompted to look into Piaget's book themselves for the full detail of his actual experimental situations, and the stimulus and starting-points which these might provide.

3. THE ODD QUESTION OF EDUCATION IN LOGIC
AGAIN: PERHAPS NOT SO UNPRACTICAL AFTER ALL?

What now, finally, of that other, so unaccustomed question of *logic?* To attempt to deal adequately with this large unfamiliar topic would require a volume to itself. But, by way of the briefest look at the lie of the land, let me suppose that such a volume came to exist and were called, for example, "Logic for the Primary School", or "Logical Thinking for Juniors". The bare word "logic" would surely be enough to frighten everyone off the whole enterprise, or else would cause them to treat it as just another of those crank ideas, to be dismissed with derision. Would this not, however, be a case of being stopped by literally a mere sound-barrier, which in fact we must learn to break through? After all, the word "logic" is not more Greek than that other Greek word "arithmetic" and for that matter, nothing like so long. We have simply become used to the latter, and to everything that goes with it. That may be the whole difference, and I have already suggested grounds why logic may be not less entitled, nor less suited, to assume the same familiar mien. In sober fact, it makes, I believe, sense to say that arithmetic is much the more sophisticated and artificial thought-formation of the two.

It is true that, according to Piaget himself and also the evidence of earlier reasoning and absurdity tests, children do not seem generally ready for strictly logical thinking until around 11–14 years. But that again could merely be due, as I have already suggested, to our past educational attitudes and assumptions, together with the limitations of traditional "logic" itself. In effect there is ample proof available that children *are* capable of cogent logical criticism and logical construction, in favourable surroundings, at far earlier ages. They are continually led to the one or the other if they live in an atmosphere that encourages them to discuss, argue and reason. And above all if this joins on to their usual lively interest in everything around them, animal, vegetable or mineral, mechanical, electrical, and so on, and if they are constantly stimulated to explore and question, to try to think up and test out suppositions or hypotheses, or to seek explanations.

A book like Susan Isaacs's *Intellectual Growth in Young Children* is full of examples of the way in which this natural development in logic works, both critically and constructively, in children down to 4–6 years. Most of those in her school were admittedly above average in intelligence, but according to normal psychological theory one might reasonably expect more average children who were only, say, a couple of years older, to show up similarly *in similar situations*. The key however would be in the real similarity of the situations—that is, they would have had to be all the way through equally stimulating to free and productive activity, with hand, eye and brain. It is not indeed even certain that under such conditions 4–6 years might not prove something like the typical commencing age for the genuine logical interests of children at large.

That is perhaps the right context in which the suggested place of logic in our educational theory should come in. I cannot try to develop this theme any further here. I only want to suggest that it may be *capable* of quite important development; and that it merits thinking about all the more just because it is so novel and unfamiliar and even repugnant to most of our past habits of thought. It may well be these habits of thought that need our fresh attention.

One point more: Of course even books on Arithmetic for the Primary School may come to look distinctly different from the way they do at present if Professor Piaget's work has the value and pregnancy which I am attributing to it. Thus we can draw no conclusions from the pattern of our current arithmetics to a parallel pattern of any hypothetical "Logic for the Primary School". On the other hand we should possibly find that if gradually we develop new types

of arithmetical text-books aiming directly at the structural
and functional growth of children's own ideas of number and
number operations, the need for a largely parallel type of
text-book of logic and logical operations would emerge at the
same time. The two directions of advance might in fact prove
to have much in common all the way through. Children
would be continually exercising and developing two comple-
mentary sets of working rules governing the activity of their
own minds and determining their efficacy and practical success. In each case they would have the same strong natural
interest in playing or working at these rules because, under
"activity" conditions, they are constantly cropping up in
everything the child does, and because things so obviously go
wrong if he falls down on them, but go so well and swim-
mingly if he masters them. The most piquant fact here is that,
as I have already suggested, the strictly logical type of interest develops earlier and more strongly than the numerical
one (apart from the first mechanical and meaningless game
of counting), as can be seen, *inter alia*, from a sufficiently
careful study of children's "Why" questions*; so that suitable forms of "Logic for Small Children" may well in the end
have far more help to give to arithmetic than vice versa.

Anyway, it does not seem impossible that on this double
foundation teachers may in future be able to build up a
groundwork of essential intellectual education far more effective and far more capable of further growth by its own re-
sources and momentum than we have known hitherto.
Whether this might not now be achievable is the largest question, or perhaps prospect, raised by the new horizons which
Piaget's work has opened up.

* I have tried to bring this out in my examination of such questions in
Susan Isaacs's *Intellectual Growth in Young Children*.

BIBLIOGRAPHY

Jean Piaget	*The Child's Conception of Number*	Routledge and Kegan Paul 1952 (*First published in French 1941*)
Eileen Churchill	*Counting and Measuring*	Routledge and Kegan Paul 1961
Z. P. Dienes	*Building up Mathematics*	Hutchinson Educational 1960
Evelyn Lawrence, T. R. Theakston, N. Isaacs	*Some Aspects of Piaget's Work*	National Froebel Foundation 1955
K. Lovell	*The Growth of Basic Mathematical and Scientific Concepts in Children*	University of London Press 1961
F. W. Land	*New Approaches to Mathematics Teaching*	Macmillan 1963

Report prepared for the Mathematical Association

	The Teaching of Mathematics in Primary Schools	G. Bell & Sons 1956

PUBLISHER'S BIBLIOGRAPHY

BOOKS BY JEAN PIAGET

Biology and Knowledge, University of Chicago Press, 1971

Child's Conception of Movement and Speed, Basic Books, 1969; Ballantine Books, 1970 (paper)

Child's Conception of Number, Humanities Press, 1964; W. W. Norton, 1965 (paper)

Child's Conception of Physical Causality (originally pub. 1930), Humanities Press, 1966; Littlefield, Adams, 1965 (paper)

Child's Conception of the World, Humanities Press, 1964; Littlefield, Adams, 1969 (paper)

Child's Conception of Time, Basic Books, 1970; Ballantine Books, 1971 (paper)

Construction of Reality in the Child, trans. by Margaret Cook, Basic Books, 1954; Ballantine Books, 1971 (paper)

Genetic Epistemology, trans. by Eleanor Duckworth, Columbia University Press, 1970; W. W. Norton, 1971 (paper)

Insights and Illusions of Philosophy, World Publishing, Meridian Books, 1971

John Amos Comenius on Education, Teachers College Press, Columbia University, 1968

Judgement and Reasoning in the Child (originally pub. 1928), Humanities Press, 1947; Littlefield, Adams, 1968 (paper)

Language and Thought of the Child (originally pub. 1959), Humanities Press, 1962; World Publishing Co., 1955 (paper)

Mechanisms of Perception, trans. by G. N. Seagrin, Basic Books, 1969

Moral Judgment of the Child, The Free Press, 1932

On the Development of Memory and Identity, Barre Publishers, 1968

Origins of Intelligence in Children, trans. by Margaret Cook, International Universities Press, 1966; W. W. Norton, 1963 (paper)

Play, Dreams & Imitation in Childhood, W. W. Norton, 1962

Psychology and Epistemology, trans. by Arnold Rosin, Grossman Publishers, 1971

Psychology of Intelligence, Humanities Press; Littlefield, Adams, 1968 (paper)

Science of Education and the Psychology of the Child, The Viking Press, 1971

Six Psychological Studies, Elkind, David, ed., Random House, 1968

Structuralism, Basic Books, 1970; Harper & Row, 1971 (paper)

with Fraisse, Paul and Reuchlin, Maurice, *Experimental Psychology: Its Scope and Method, Vol 1, History & Methods,* Basic Books, 1968

with Inhelder, Barbel, *Child's Conception of Space,* Humanities Press, 1963; W. W. Norton, 1967 (paper)

———— *Early Growth of Logic in the Child,* Humanities Press, 1971; W. W. Norton, 1969 (paper)

———— *Growth of Logical Thinking From Childhood to Adolescence: An Essay on the Construction of Formal Operational Structure,* Basic Books, 1958

———— *Psychology of the Child,* trans. by Helen Weaver, Basic Books, 1969

with Inhelder, Barbel, and Szeminska, Alina, *Child's Conception of Geometry,* trans. by E. A. Lunzer, Basic Books, 1960

BOOKS ABOUT PIAGETIAN PSYCHOLOGY

Almy, Millie, et al., *Young Children's Thinking: Studies of Some Aspects of Piaget's Theory,* Teachers College Press, Columbia University, 1966

Beard, Ruth M., *Outline of Piaget's Developmental Psychology for Students and Teachers,* Basic Books, 1969

Boyle, D. J., *Students' Guide to Piaget,* Pergamon Press, 1969

Brearley, Molly and Hitchfield, Elizabeth, *Guide to Reading Piaget,* Schocken Books, 1969

Brearley, Molly, ed., *Teaching of Young Children: Some Applications of Piaget's Learning Theory,* Schocken Books, 1970

Copeland, Richard W., *How Children Learn Mathematics: Teaching Implications of Piaget's Research,* The Macmillan Co., 1970

Elkind, David, *Children and Adolescents: Interpretive Essays on Jean Piaget,* Oxford University Press, 1971

Flavell, John H., *Development Psychology of Jean Piaget,* Van Nostrand Reinhold, 1963

Furth, Hans G., *Piaget and Knowledge: Theoretical Foundations,* Prentice-Hall, 1969

———— *Piaget for Teachers,* Prentice-Hall, 1970

Ginsburg, Herbert and Opper, Silvia, eds., *Piaget's Theory of Intellectual Development: An Introduction,* Prentice-Hall, 1969

Gouin Decarie, Therese, *Intelligence and Affectivity in Early Childhood: An Experimental Study of Jean Piaget's Object Concept and Object Relations,* International Universities Press, 1966

Helmore, G. A., *Piaget: A Practical Consideration,* Pergamon Press, 1970

Kessen, W. and Kuhlman, Clementina, eds., *Thought in the Young Child,* Kraus Reprint, 1962

Kohnstamm, Geldolph A., *Piaget's Analysis of Class Inclusion: Right or Wrong,* Humanities Press, 1967

Laurendeau, Monique and Pinard, Adrien, *Development of the Concept of Space in the Child,* International Universities Press, 1970

Maier, Henry W., *Three Theories of Child Development,* Harper & Row, 1969

Phillips, John L., Jr., *Origins of Intellect: Piaget's Theory,* W. H. Freeman, 1969

Pulaski, Mary A., *Understanding Piaget: An Introduction to Children's Cognitive Development,* Harper & Row, 1971.

Richmond, P. G., *Introduction to Piaget,* Basic Books, 1971

Wadsworth, Burry J., *Piaget's Theory of Cognitive Development: An Introduction for Students of Psychology and Education,* David McKay, 1971

Wolff, Peter H., *Developmental Psychologies of Jean Piaget and Psychoanalysis,* International Universities Press, 1960